A Wiley Brand

FEARLESS FACILITATION

The Ultimate Field Guide to Engaging (and Involving!) Your Audience

Cyndi Maxey, CSP, and Kevin E. O'Connor, CSP

WILEY

Cover design by J. Puda
Maxey photo by Rick Mitchell
O'Connor photo by Steve Ewert

Published by Pfeiffer

An Imprint of Wiley
One Montgomery Street, Suite 1200, San Francisco, CA 94104-4594

www.pfeiffer.com

For additional copies/bulk purchases of this book in the U.S. please contact 800-274-4434.

Pfeiffer books and products are available through most bookstores. To contact Pfeiffer directly call our
Customer Care Department within the U.S. at 800-274-4434, outside the U.S. at 317-572-3985,
fax 317-572-4002, or visit www.pfeiffer.com.

Pfeiffer publishes in a variety of print and electronic formats and by print-on-demand. Some material
included with standard print versions of this book may not be included in e-books or in print-on-
demand. If this book refers to media such as a CD or DVD that is not included in the version you pur-
chased, you may download this material at http://booksupport.wiley.com. For more information about
Wiley products, visit www.wiley.com.

Library of Congress Cataloging-in-Publication Data

Maxey, Cyndi.
    Fearless facilitation : the ultimate field guide to engaging (and involving!) your audience /
Cyndi Maxey and Kevin O'Connor.
        pages cm
    Includes index.
    ISBN 978-1-118-37581-5 (pbk.); 978-1-118-41750-8 (ebk.);
    978-1-118-42061-4 (ebk.); 978-1-118-56651-0 (ebk.)
        1. Business presentations   2. Business communication.   I. O'Connor, Kevin, 1947- II. Title.
HF5718.22.M328   2013
658.4'52—dc23
                                                                                        2013001289

Acquiring Editor: Matthew Davis	Editor: Rebecca Taff
Director of Development: Kathleen Dolan Davies	Editorial Assistant: Ryan Noll
Developmental Editor: Susan Rachmeler	Manufacturing Supervisor: Becky Morgan
Production Editor: Michael Kay	Printed in the United States of America

PB Printing 10 9 8 7 6 5 4 3 2 1

To my Chicago neighbors, who have fearlessly facilitated lifelong friendships and steadfast support of my work.
Cyndi Maxey

For Ross Keane, who taught and modeled facilitation for and with me, and to Howard and LouEllen Horwitz for letting me do it!
Kevin O'Connor

Contents

Preface

OVER THE PAST TEN YEARS, we have collaborated on books and articles that explored and documented our love of communication, presentation, and leadership. We have facilitated countless workshops together and coached and developed presenters and leaders who were on the same team. Associations like American Society for Training and Development (ASTD) and National Speakers Association (NSA) provided opportunities for us to speak about our work and create new ideas along the way.

The idea for this book began with a presentation we called "Fearless Facilitation" at the 2009 NSA conference; the intent was to encourage professional speakers to "let loose" and let the audience in. The response was positive, and so we continued to perfect the concept of "fearlessness" while involving a group. We delivered new, expanded versions of the presentation for trainers and leaders at the ASTD international conferences of 2010 and 2011 and then proposed the idea to Pfeiffer as a potential book. This is our fourth book together, and we are honored you are reading it.

Many times leaders and presenters can be so wrapped up in what they say and what is on their slides that they wait until the very end to state: "We have a few moments for questions." This is a tremendous mistake and a disservice to audiences who really do want to talk and not just be "talked at." We offer this book to you in the same light.

Be fearless and let your audience in!

Cyndi Maxey and Kevin E. O'Connor
Chicago, Illinois
Fall 2012

Acknowledgments

A BOOK IDEA NEVER COMES to print with a respected publishing house without the inspiration and support of many people.

To begin, we would like to thank Mark Morrow for his professionalism, enthusiasm, and wise connection to Pfeiffer/Wiley; Matt Davis for his belief in us and the theme and the audience for this book; and our agent, Jay Poynor, for representing us with caring attention and wisdom for the past ten years.

We would also like to thank our great families for their interest and support: Ryan Maxey, Phelan Maxey, Corbbmacc O'Connor, Lanty O'Connor, and Rita O'Connor. We love you and appreciate your enthusiasm for our writing careers.

Finally, we are grateful to all who contributed stories, interviews, poetry, or experiences to make this book "come alive" with professional applicability: Leon Adcock; Therry Adcock; Dianna Booher; Dennis DeBondt; Loren Ekroth, Ph.D.; Walter Eppich, MD, M.Ed.; Linus Erkenswick; Fred

Friedman, JD; Randy Gage; Georgia Gove; Bob Gilbert; Ken Johnson, Pharm.D.; Dr. Alan Kaplan, MD; Madalyn Kenney; Dr. Mehmood Khan, MD; Diane Kubal; Helen Meldrum, Ph.D.; Kay Minger; Dr. Domeena Renshaw, MD; Miriella Saucedo-Marquez; Kenny Sevara; Terry Sheeler; Bryan Silbermann, CAE; Jane Sweeney; Ricky C. Tanksley; and Dr. John Vozenilek, MD.

Thanks also to editorial support from Corbbmacc O'Connor, O'Consulting Group, Alexandria, Virginia and to the animated illustrations throughout from Robert Parker, student at Columbia College Chicago.

About the Authors

CYNDI MAXEY, CSP, (MA, Northwestern University, communication studies) has owned Maxey Creative Inc., a communication training and consulting firm, since 1989. She is a professional speaker and coach, and she holds the Certified Speaking Professional designation awarded by the National Speakers Association, held by fewer than three hundred women internationally. A career-long member of the American Society for Training and Development (ASTD) and a leader in ASTD's Chicago chapter, she has spoken frequently at ASTD international conferences on presentations, training, and communication.

She works most often with healthcare, insurance, consumer products, women's, and medical audiences in communication, presentations, and facilitation. Maxey is a past president of the National Speakers Association's Illinois chapter, and she was the recipient of NSA Illinois' Humanitarian of the Year 2009 for her volunteer work with fundraising events for schools, churches, and the community.

Maxey has co-authored five books on presentations and communication. She lives in Chicago, Illinois, where her grown children and Labrador retriever, Max Maxey, provide both balance and chaos in her life.

KEVIN E. O'CONNOR, CSP, is a speaker, consultant, and teacher specializing in working with medical and scientific professionals charged with leading their peers as well as with teams of professionals collaborating over projects in a matrix environment. He specializes in teaching professionals to have influence and impact over those who may not directly report to them, even those who may not even want to be influenced!

O'Connor teaches graduate and undergraduate classes at Chicago's Loyola University, Columbia College of Chicago, and at specific gatherings of professional groups, including corporate executives, physician executives, healthcare leaders, and teams of professionals in the United States, Canada, England, and Dubai.

O'Connor is a Certified Speaking Professional. Currently fewer than 550 persons in the world hold this honor for speaking and teaching excellence. He has three master's degrees and is the author or co-author of seven books. He lives in the northwest suburbs of Chicago.

Introduction

WELCOME, AND WE HOPE OUR title drew you to the words herein. We're glad you want to be fearless, and we're especially glad your interest is facilitation! Fearless is a strong word, perhaps even a strange word, to describe this skill of facilitation that, by definition, means "to make easy." Yet, many facilitators today are full of fear. They are wary of stopping talking, stopping their slide show, or departing from their agenda in order to find out what their people really think, feel, and are prepared to do.

They fear because they don't know how. They fear out of a misplaced sense of what excellence is. They fear that somehow their adult audience will either not participate or will hijack their meeting. Nothing could be further from the truth. Adults require two things in order to learn: they want to feel included and connected. This is never accomplished by lecture, silence, slide decks, or a tight agenda that permits nothing but lifeless "yeses."

Leading and facilitating a meeting, event, training session, or webinar to a successful outcome is a challenging task for even the most talented of facilitators. Beyond the painful detail of agenda planning, there is no guarantee how people will react or participate until they tell us through their behavior. Some people relish being involved and contributing; others don't. Some arrive with negative preconceived notions, while others are open to anything, as long as it's interesting at the moment to them!

To add to the challenge, growing numbers of meetings, events, and training sessions are being held online, on the phone, and in chat formats, making it difficult to simply monitor the audience, let alone involve them!

Each Chapter in This Book Will Open Your Eyes . . .

. . . to terms and techniques you may not have encountered before, such as organic facilitation, breaking the fourth wall between you and the audience, tapping into the natural resources of the group, how conversation and facilitation skills intertwine, how to work with a largely introverted professional population, setting up activities "gently," how to "listen live" as a talk show host does, how to "go with it" as the improvisation artist learns, what groups of six and six hundred have in common, what a ninety-one-year-old nursing home resident knows about audience needs, how to use the experts among you, how to avoid "death by committee," how to operate from a mindset of "experience not content," special strategies for volunteers, and special strategies for audiences of one gender, culture, or age group.

This is neither a book of games or techniques, nor is it a theoretical academic volume. Rather, we strive to unite theory and activity, engage the facilitator with the audience, and create memories that result in enthusiasm and action. Chapter One, "Heard on the Street," provides some useful definitions and general "rules of thumb" that apply throughout. After reading Chapter One, you may wish to skip around. Note that at the end of every chapter there are specific Coach's Comments, which address frequently asked questions from real people. Also make note of the Appendices, which include additional tips, activities, and tools.

This Book Is for You If . . .

. . . you're a training professional, training director, training manager, training specialist, or organization development manager who trains others for behavior change. You may train the trainers, consult with the organization, and coach and support. Your job is to make a tangible difference in how others do their jobs.

. . . you're a corporate or association leader who is charged with planning, leading, and facilitating meetings at work. We will help you fearlessly involve people. You may be a seasoned professional who "knows the team knows," but has no idea how to persuade them to voice their honest responses. Or you may be an emerging leader who is intensely aware that lecture, slide decks, and constricted agendas are a thing of the past. You will relate to the stories herein of a range of corporate and business professionals—from a VP in information technology to an oncology nurse manager; from the team leader for lab technicians to a senior supervisor in telecommunications customer service.

. . . you're a student of human education and development. You will find this book a valuable resource for your courses related to presentations, training, leadership, management, public relations, marketing, corporate communication, advertising, business, and more. It will not only help you with these topics, but it also provides good tips for you on how to involve people in the meetings, study groups, and presentations that are a part of your student life.

. . . you're a volunteer leader in your community, school, or charitable organization. If you're responsible for leading meetings that encourage and motivate others in a volunteer environment, you will find many ideas that are easy to apply.

. . . you're a religious leader who addresses the crowd and motivates your staff and members.

. . . you're an entrepreneur looking for new ways to make an impact.

. . . you're a creative person making your living in the arts looking for help energizing your audiences and marketing your talents.

This Book Will Help You Plan
Every Meeting You Lead

You will learn to put audience mindset top of mind, beginning every meeting with an immediately involving activity or discussion that unifies the group. You will be able to locate the key points in the meeting to facilitate and involve, rather than just lecture and present information. You will gain confidence and be able to use easy-to-implement facilitative techniques with any type of participant (job role, level, background, gender, culture, attitude) and follow up with clarity and speed.

In short, this book goes beyond a simplistic listing of tactics and techniques. Rather, it teaches how to think about how others learn, how they change their minds, how they say "yes" to a concept or initiative, and how they decide, change, and develop.

Congratulations on your commitment to fearless facilitation.

One

Heard on the Street

The Audience Does Know!

"I want them walking out of my office feeling better than when they walked in."
—*Mehmood Khan, MD, FACE; CEO, Global Nutrition Group; SVP and*
Chief Science Officer, PepsiCo

- Audience involvement results in audience satisfaction, significant learning, and achieved outcomes.

- Facilitator fearlessness begins with courage to lead from personal power, not superiority.

- Fearless facilitation is a courageous activity for both the speaker and the audience.

The Audience Doesn't Lie

If you have ever been in charge of a meeting, training session, or event of any kind, you know how great it feels to have everyone as excited and involved as you are. Those are the meetings people talk about later—in a good way! Those are the meetings that are remembered when people are promoted. Those are the meetings that truly inspire change and productive work relationships. Yet, sadly, most meetings don't garner such rave reviews and results. Instead, what's more commonly "heard on the street" or in the parking lot afterward is that the meeting was a waste of time. People feel that their energy and mental capacity were undermined and underestimated. Admittedly, how many times have you yourself proclaimed, "What a waste of time!" "I already saw those slides." or "She read the slides. Next time, just e-mail me." or "His meetings are always the same . . . B-O-R-I-N-G!" or "I stopped listening about an hour into the training. I was so confused."

Time, energy, and mental capacity are not small considerations. And yet, most presenters avoid involving others when they have the floor. Why is that? What is fearful about facilitation? How can one be more fearless? First, to clarify, let's define some terms:

> *Facilitator:* one who helps to bring about an outcome (for example learning, productivity, or communication) by providing indirect or unobtrusive assistance, guidance, or supervision.

Think about the last time a presenter opened the discussion up for everyone, and then made it easy for everyone to participate. That's facilitation. When we see a ballet, enjoy a comedy routine, hear a sixteen-year-old Judy Garland sing "Over the Rainbow," or watch Gene Kelly dance in the rain, we are astonished at how effortlessly they perform. Yet, their actions are the result of painstaking practice, gifted talent, and specific skills that come together to make for classic moments in our lives. Successful facilitation is much the same. The best facilitators look as if they are doing so with no effort, with little movement, and on the spur of the moment. In truth, these facilitators are at the peak of their skill, just as the performers are. But not everyone knows the skills, practices relentlessly, or is able to command competence with such ease.

Kevin had a group of dentists and dental students in a wine bar (yes, we are not kidding!) for a meeting about mentoring for three hours. (The wine came later.) The venue was not perfect, but it did attract dental students, which was the heart of the reason for the meeting. Kevin's goal was not to teach mentoring, but to have them experience mentoring, to meet one another, to talk, and to have a positive experience with one another. He wanted the younger and more experienced students to build connections with one another.

Therefore, he made a decision early on that connection, not content, was the king of this meeting. He prepared four mini-lecturettes and interspersed them with groups of two and three speaking to one another about the topic at hand.

After the seminar, the host said, "Today I met ten people I did not know . . . that's what I came for!"

Be aware when connection trumps content, and then get out of the way!

For many presenters, it is much easier (and seemingly safer) to keep talking. When have you felt safe to say what you wanted to say (and what needed to be said) in a meeting? Too often, it feels safer to just say nothing. Nothing said, nothing noted.

> *Fearless:* possessing or displaying courage; able to face and deal with danger or fear without flinching; invulnerable to fear or intimidation; audacious.

Presenters, participants, and leaders who facilitate well are fearless, because they give up the traditional control of an audience or of a team and allow the other to talk, question, and disagree. While this may not seem like a big deal, consider the last time you knew that what you were planning to say would be challenged, disagreed with, or even met with a caustic remark. How did you feel? More to the point, how did you proceed?

> *Acts of courage:* when you let your audience talk to you, when you seek input from your team, when you ask your boss (or your administrative assistant) for advice.

Those who keep talking take the safe route. Those who facilitate the conversation take the courageous route. These courageous ones act—not without risk, of course—and for that, they are "fearless" in our book. "Fearless" facilitation results in "flavorful" responses and outcomes. Diane Kubal, founder of Fulcrum Network, a consultant referral network specializing in training and organization development, auditions many presenters and trainers before she puts them before her clients. They present a mini-module of their typical approach to a topic. She has noticed that "a lot of training and human resource people are doing the same thing. I'm looking for a flavor other than vanilla." Fearless facilitation is one important ingredient for adding flavor.

Think back to your last meeting. Did the presenter talk, talk, talk, and then at the very end say, "Any questions?" (Some even add the nonverbal look that says, "I hope not!") Socrates learned in ancient Greece that asking questions engaged learners. He also learned that it was not always well received by others who preferred to lecture. While it is said that it cost him his life, these days we believe the reverse is true: talk, talk, and more talk makes you indistinguishable from your colleagues and your competition. You become vanilla.

- Dare to be different, even in small ways:
  - Don't read your slides, ever.
  - Form the audience into discussion groups early.
  - Be simple and direct. Complex directions will not be well understood. Ask them to do one thing at a time.
  - Remove the traditional outline slide and speak to needs instead. Throw some meat out to the audience with a bold statement that will make them respond internally with, "This is worth listening to!"
  - Move around the room early and often. Move physically close to your audience.
- Lighten up your presentations:
  - Don't be afraid of humor; just never tell jokes.
  - Present in metaphors as well as in a data format.
  - Consider different kinds of snacks and drinks.
  - Consider not using PowerPoint when it is expected.
  - Become the master of teaching with a flip chart or whiteboard.

- Consider yourself a teacher, not a presenter. Model your style after your favorite teacher.
- Really engage with your audience early and often:
  - Meet and greet.
  - Talk with them on breaks.
  - One-on-one during breaks or discussions, ask whether they are "doing OK" frequently. They will often respond with encouragement for you, which will help you stay on track.
- Prepare your audience for something that is extraordinarily "out of the ordinary":
  - A leap of movement from one way of being to another
  - A creative meeting environment
  - Different kinds of food for meals or breaks
  - Interview a special guest (CEO, trustee, local leader) in front of the group.
- Develop an internal routine, unseen by the audience:
  - Cyndi always walks into the audience no matter what the content or how large the room.
  - Kevin always begins with a story, usually three, to set the tone; then the audience is put into pairs to discuss a relevant question, then groups of three. This is standard for him.
- Be ready to move, fall back, surge, and wait as needed:
  - Move when you see boredom in their eyes.
  - Fall back when they engage willingly with one another.
  - Surge when you feel more passion and energy in the group than you assumed would be there.
  - Therefore, add more of your own, move them less often and with deeper questions.
  - Wait patiently for them to tell, for them to explain, for them to summarize.

- Be conscious of your goals, your time, and your unneeded content:
  - Streamline your content.
  - Teach in "chunks" of material. Adults learn best this way.
- Never ever:
  - Race through your slides because you are short of time. No one is listening anyway. Focus on what experience they need, not what content you need.
  - Finish late. Never. Ever. Never. You will not be forgiven . . . ever!
  - Call someone out who seems not to be involved. He or she will hate you forever.
  - Think that you know more than they do. You might, but it is useless to think so. Form a learning community, not an adoration society.
  - Use a laser pointer . . . ever. It is the mark of a rank amateur, but we will be the only ones to tell you so.

It's About Time!

Facilitation is the skill of the present and of the future. Gone are the days when great presenters lectured for an hour or more. Or in your experience, are they gone? Gone, too, are the days when the presenter's questions were as they were in school—with only one right answer. Really gone? Really? Gone, too, we hope, are the days when the PowerPoint presentation was more powerful than the presenter. How about your last meeting? Perhaps these days should be gone.

If you want to assert leadership with your team and be seen as the expert, then you must learn how to facilitate a presentation (whether to one person or to one hundred people). Make conversation easy and useful, and help others think through necessary solutions rather than restating the problems we all know exist.

So How Do You Begin?

- Know the "real" reason for the meeting and the "real" outcome desired.

- Prepare short mini-lectures that address content but are short enough to allow for more interaction. Adult learning research says that "chunking" material, breaking it down into its component parts, is one of the best ways to convey complex information.

- Assertively put the audience into small groups of two or three, with the following notice: "Please find a partner who is not the one sitting next to you, and have a seat."

  - This is all it will take to get the room buzzing.

  - Then give them a topic and a time to talk.

  - When finished, somehow recover the data so all hear.

  - Trust that the audience knows more than you do.

Recognize and understand that to facilitate is not easy work. It is easier to prepare and deliver a PowerPoint presentation, beginning with: "I'll take questions at the end." It's far easier to start a discussion when you know the answers. Leaving a voicemail message that spells out precisely what we want without creating a connection or engaging the other is just as easy, also.

The world of entrepreneurial work and the world of organizations are replete with examples of control, fear, authority, and organizational correctness. How often have you stayed quiet at a meeting when you knew your contribution would not be well received? How often do you see junior staff struggling to obey, conform, and do whatever is perceived as right in order to gain favor and to move ahead? How often are mistakes feared and—when they are made—blame is the order of the day, not learning, not alternatives, not reassurance, and certainly not encouragement.

We believe this need not be.

It All Begins with Courage

You can be a change agent in a transformative and still subtle way that allows for you to be a "stealth facilitator" where your impact will be felt, things will be different, people will change, and they will not know how, when, why, or who. They will only know "something is different here."

It all begins, of course, with courage. The Viennese psychiatrist Alfred Adler once remarked that if he were to give a child any personality characteristic, it would be courage, for with courage, "one can combat life's greatest problem, which is fear."

How then is fear manifested where you work? How do you see fear play out in simple day-to-day situations? How does fear manifest itself in you? Do you become quiet? Dig in your heels? Ignore? Fight? Resent?

Do you recognize the fear behind excessive perfectionism or authoritarian demands; in departmental combat or in a deafening silence; in thoughtless conformity or group think? Regardless of fear's manifestation, the danger is that we can live and work in a situation that constricts rather than elicits from, that concerns itself with transactions rather than transformations, and that forces us to tap down the potential of our people rather than tap the talent that lives within them. As you muster your courage, consider these three keys to begin the work of facilitating "fearlessly" wherever you go.

Three Keys to Facilitate Fearlessly
First, Remember That Your Goal Is to Be of Value to Others

If you see others as merely a path to what you want, it quickly becomes clear that you, not they, are the important ones. This is not a strong way to start.

Have you ever sat in the audience of a presenter who asked questions, seemingly to help the audience understand? Soon it became clear that what mattered was that the audience was supposed to give only the "right" answers. This form of teaching is common in traditional university classrooms and many professional schools. It encourages conformity, promotes discouragement, and often heightens a fear of embarrassment. As the audience offers up ideas, you can spot the presenter using this style because he keeps saying, "Not quite . . . no . . . pretty close. I guess no one knows this!" What becomes clear is that value is defined by what the presenter sees as valuable, not the audience's experience or feedback.

The fearless facilitator focuses on value as defined by others.

Every person in your audience and on your team wants only one thing: to have his or her problem solved. Even the most loving, caring, other-focused person wants exactly the same thing that the most selfish, narcissistic, obnoxious person on your team wants: the problem solved. This is the true meaning of value. We often hear the term "value proposition" in business today as if we know what will fulfill our customers. What we propose to them is to seek their "yes." What if, however, we had a "value conversation" with them instead. What if we listened? What if we asked? What if we saw value as they saw it: Can you help me?

Think about your next office conversation. Do you (or your colleague) focus on the other person or do you simply engage in a mutual monologue? Listen closely next time. Does your conversational partner talk about you or about him- or herself? How about you? Who is your focus?

The fearless facilitator paraphrases, summarizes, and empathizes in order to stay close with the topic of the other person.

If you master only three skills, these are the platinum standards. For it is with these seemingly simple skills that you will connect with the other, understand where to go next, and set yourself apart. Each of these skills is often misunderstood and misused. Be careful to understand and to use them with care, but also with courage.

Paraphrasing is not parroting. Parroting is repeating the exact same words that the other person used. This is annoying to them and can be terribly embarrassing to you, simply because most people will loudly proclaim, "Hello! I just said that!"

Paraphrasing is the skill of listening carefully to the other and then, in your own words, summarizing as closely as possible the essence of what the other meant. For example, imagine that a participant declares, "I really learned the most from the bad bosses I had, y'know the ones who looked over your shoulder all the time and wanted things 'their way or the highway.'" Your paraphrase might be, "So you remember what the bad bosses did and how you learned from that?"

Summarizing is a bit different. When you summarize, you can even announce that you are doing so. (You don't want to do that with paraphrasing; it is bad form and will knock you both off of your flow!) When you summarize, you are taking the content of the other person and arranging it in a way that presents it for his or her approval and perhaps continued presentation of his or her thoughts. In the example with the participant who remembered bad bosses, your summary may sound something like this: "So bad bosses taught you not to micro-manage and not to force people to do things one way only?"

What distinguishes summarizing from paraphrasing is that it is content-rich and is a cooperative activity between you and the other person. Paraphrasing is a process of listening. The metaphor that may explain the difference is to imagine you are walking with the other in the woods and as you walk you are listening to the other describe the journey (paraphrasing); then you both come to a clearing in the woods and stop and pull out a map and a compass (summarizing).

Empathizing adds emotion into the mix. Here you are listening closely and are aware of the feeling the person has as he or she is speaking to you and you add this to the mix of either paraphrasing or summarizing. Again referring to the example of the participant with the bad boss, an empathizing response may be, "Sounds like the discomfort you felt as a result of a bad boss's choices stuck with you."

The point here for the fearless facilitator is that you have to be relentlessly focused on the other person. This is clearly countercultural both in business and in our social circles today. This week pay attention to how many people talk about themselves and how few ask you, care to ask you, care at all about you! When you facilitate, you have to be completely, authentically, totally with the other person. The rewards for doing so are tremendous. Failure to do so means you are too ready to use the hackneyed, pedestrian, Neanderthal phrase, "Any questions?"

Does "group discussion" mean being stuck at a table with the same people for the entire meeting and discussing issues that the presenter poses, rather than ideas dreamed up by the group?

The fearless facilitator eliminates the tables!

You will know you are a grown-up facilitator when you can ask for and move the tables out of the room! Round tables are the bane of good conversation. Move what separates us out of the room in which you really want some good conversation. This is a standard in many meetings: round tables, big tables, huge tables, U-shaped tables, wooden ones with impressive pads, electricity, and speakers coming from underneath . . . yikes, no wonder nobody talks, they are too busy being insulated from one another!

Be prepared for the most common question we hear when we make this request: "Where will I put my stuff?" We reply, "Great question! On the floor, over there, away from us!" Stuff will separate us, too! Fearless facilitators let the audience go "tech naked," nothing to get in the way of really connecting.

Tables discourage focused conversations, important talks, and deeper meaning. Take away the tables and move people around the room in groups of two or three, sometimes four (no more), and watch what happens to the conversation. The dynamic here is an important one. Do you want your audience to be involved participants or judgmental observers? Think about the last time you were listening to a lecture. Even with the best of presenters, when it is a one-way conversation, our job as the audience is to listen and perhaps take notes, then take some action (or not!) afterward. In a participatory presentation, however, we become active learners. It is our contention that the world of meetings is moving dramatically more toward an involved audience.

Dr. John Vozenilek, founder of the simulation lab at Northwestern University's Feinberg School of Medicine in Chicago, speaks of the excitement he feels when he teaches in the simulation lab: "I love the look in [the students'] eyes when they 'get' it. This happens more in the lab than in the classroom, much more." Audience members are often preprogrammed to accept the traditional passive role, but beware, even the friendliest audiences are judging your presentation. Involved audiences—the ones you allow and encourage to interact with one another and with you—are your fellow presenters and fellow learners.

The fearless facilitator knows that more learning happens in the "lab" environment.

Second, Remember That Others Value Those Who Can Help Them

You do not instinctively value those who are smarter, better, or say they are. You value what you value. You are the value interpreter. This may seem like common sense, but consider how some experts treat you, your teams, or audiences. Some consider themselves the fuel filling up the empty gas tanks . . . us! The mindset you use when presenting is vital, for it determines the technique and strategy.

How you approach others signifies how you regard them, value them, and will impact them. Have you ever felt talked down to? How quickly do you recognize this is happening? This is called vertical communication, with the superior one on top and the inferior one on the bottom. This has been a traditional teaching technique for physicians in residency, where they are grilled by the senior doctor, often feeling less than, humiliated, or worse! (The television show "House," where the doctor ensures that at all times his residents know he is smarter, is an example of vertical communication.)

The fearless facilitator speaks on a horizontal plane of equality, never on the vertical plane of superiority.

We want you to be strong; not superior. Strength is a quality of the individual; superiority is the myth we believe about ourselves in treating someone else without respect. If you work from your strengths, you will never have to work to be better than, over another, or diminish anyone, even a rival who is attempting to be superior to you. You may not be able to "kill with kindness," but you sure can neutralize with it.

Fearless facilitators know that if they can encourage the other to articulate what he or she thinks, feels, and knows, then the facilitator will be in a better position to teach, discuss, and interact with mutual respect. To do this, however, means you give up your natural urge to be on top. You become willing to listen, to really hear, and perhaps to learn yourself. Fearless facilitators who work on the horizontal plane learn something new every day, even about the areas in which they are experts.

At a lecture, have you ever felt you were being "fed" by the person with the "food" and what you thought had no bearing on the encounter? Some lectures are highly entertaining, some less so, and others are boring, tedious, and distancing . . . no matter how smart the lecturer.

Lecturing is easy when you think about it. You don't even need a class or an audience in front of you. You only require your own ears. This can be seen every day in law, medical, pharmacy, and business schools around the country. You will also find lecturing in schools from first grade through high school. Somehow and somewhere we mis-learned that talking has a teaching effect. Socrates showed us how questions and dialogue are the real stuff of learning, as long as they are done with respect and do not become an opportunity to show our (assumed) superiority.

> The fearless facilitator recognizes that lecturing can be the easy way out.

For some, non-participation by the team or audience is a strategy devised to keep us in our place, to obtain a silent approval, to ramrod an initiative through. This is more fearless "force-ification" than fearless facilitation. We see it in business and organizational work daily. It is organizational manipulation at its best *and* at its worst. It is deeply resented by those oppressed by it, but the power of the job, the paycheck, and the promotion allows for its continued use. One client said of his boss, "The guy is really evil, but I don't have to be around him too much, so I guess . . . ." Another said of a particularly ruthless superior, "He was just diagnosed with cancer and for that I feel bad, but at least it means light at the end of the tunnel for the rest of us." Yikes!

The fearless facilitator is alert to non-participation.

The fearless facilitator, however, leads from personal power, not from the height of superiority. This leader is willing to learn in order to lead, willing to listen in order to be heard, and willing to wait in order to move forward. In short, this leader who is a fearless facilitator knows that mutual respect is at the heart of every human interaction. As human beings, we instantly recognize when we are respected and when we are not. More than being liked, being powerful, being admired, and being right, we want to be respected; we are that type of being. The fearless facilitator not only knows this but acts this way. You can see it practiced in his or her every move.

The fearless facilitator is respectful, first and foremost.

Third, You Help Others Most When Your Focus Is on Them

Ironically, when you focus so clearly on others, this is precisely when you get what you want from your interaction with them. You cannot focus on others in order to receive; you only receive when your focus is on them for them. This is an important distinction—a very important distinction.

It is quite easy and natural to be concerned about ourselves. It is a remarkable event, however, when the focus from the other is on us. Can you remember the last time this happened to you at work? At home? Or anywhere?

> Fearless facilitators work to focus on others with attentiveness, questions, and interest.

They do this with one simple technique: they ask open-ended questions that cannot be answered with a "yes" or a "no." Here are some commonly used examples of open-ended questions:

- "How do you see this happening?"
- "What are your thoughts on . . .?"
- "How would you describe . . .?"
- "Why did you select this option?"
- "What is your position on this and why?"
- "What are some of the most important reasons for . . . ."
- "How would you train a new hire in this area?"
- "What are your most common challenges?"
- "Why would we want to increase your budget?"
- "What are your team's strengths?"

As you can see, the options are nearly endless. You can ask question after open question until you find the response you and the group both need.

The fearless facilitator, regardless of technique, always shows intense interest. This facilitator will do so when he or she is not even all that interested. He or she employs one added technique: acting "as if" he or she is interested in order to be interested.

Actors do the same when summoning up strong emotion. They don't simply cry with real tears by remembering a sad event, they—as one told us recently—"assume the physical position of the sadness and the tears come." Something as simple as moving toward your audience, moving around with them, and leaning in will help you become a better facilitator. You will even appear better to the audience! Physical proximity is important because the audience wants the intimacy with you. They want you as much as they want your message.

Fearless facilitators, even in large venues, often get off the "stage" completely or from time to time in order to "meet and greet" the audience.

The famous presenter, Zig Ziglar, was known for his stage presence; he would often move down to the very edge of the stage and stoop down ever so close to his audience. When he did, they knew he was saying something very important to them. Fearless facilitators do the same, not to fake interest, but to become more interested in their audience, to have more perceived value by the audience, and to engender more for them, from them, and with them.

And on a Final and Very Important Note . . .

Fearless facilitation must be fearless for both the presenter and the participants. The presenter must take risks. The participants must not see the risks. The participants must feel safe.

A fearless facilitator's risk taking must be invisible and unnoticed.

Coach's Comments

I recently heard Doris Kearns Goodwin speak. She just stands at the podium and tells Lincoln stories, and she's brilliant! Is facilitation always necessary?

No! If you are an expert with a best-selling book, people are coming to hear you talk about your book. And . . . yes! You will still need to be a savvy facilitator before as you get to know your client's needs and after your presentation during the Q&A session. That means working with a microphone handler (if you have one), controlling questions, answering briefly with just the right amount of information, and customizing your answers to the audience as you get a feel for the types of questions they are asking. You may also be inspired with additional comments and questions based on theirs. So facilitation plays a part in every speaking engagement!

Depending on the situation, Doris may even facilitate more if she were with a cadre of other Lincoln experts debating research, approaches, or authenticity of newly discovered manuscripts. Facilitation can be in every engagement. How we use it will be dictated by what we want to accomplish.

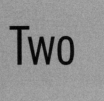

Two

Organic Facilitation

"Cooperation isn't getting people to do what you want them to do. It's getting them to want to do what you want them to do."

—Earl Nightingale

- Create a comfort level with this new skill and make it look easy. Fearless facilitators are like Montessori teachers, blending in and out of the students' awareness, ready to help, always watching, making learning natural and easy.

- Take beginning steps to add this natural, organic quality to your style. Fearless facilitators are always ready to add one more thing to their repertoire to make this and that adjustment for the benefit of their learners.

- Make facilitation valuable to the other person and to the audience. Fearless facilitators always focus on the value the other interprets: the only real value is from the learner's point of view.

What comes to mind when you think "organic"? Farmers and marketers want you to think of organic as "natural, not artificial, without additional ingredients, and pure." We'd like you to think the same thing about facilitation! When done well, an audience views facilitation as a natural, normal, and important conversation. When done poorly, it can be seen as a distraction, something artificial, added unnecessarily. When you fearlessly facilitate, the audience will know they are in good hands, with no artificial ingredients.

We were working with a coaching client, a motivational speaker, who wanted to blend more audience interaction into her presentations. Feedback from previous groups told her she needed to engage the audience more frequently, but she was challenged by her own attitude toward involvement. She revealed to us, "I really don't want to work that hard when I'm in the audience, I'd rather just sit and listen." Perhaps you feel similarly. However, if facilitation is done correctly, the audience should never feel like they're working hard. Instead, the overall tone of involvement is organic. As such, the audience is involved, not passive; enjoying, not judging; and learning, not forgetting.

We compare fearless facilitation to organic food in three ways:

1. It is less known, a bit rare, sometimes hard to find: you will be distinguished as different when you are skilled in facilitation.

2. It is seen by many as healthier in the long run: your outcomes will be more significant, the learning longer-lasting, and your audience will remember more material. Oh, and they'll remember you, too!

3. It takes time to grow and perfect: fearless facilitation is not a series of games and techniques, but rather a mindset for teaching, presenting, and speaking.

Let's take a closer look at what this means to you, the fearless facilitator.

Organic Facilitation Is Less Known

Most organically grown food is less known than other brands; sometimes it isn't branded at all. The same holds for the activities and initiatives you design for great facilitation. They are carefully customized to the program. While "off-the-shelf" games, case studies, role plays, and other activities can certainly be used well to help people learn and apply concepts, they should be selected with caution. Audiences today are quick to know when they are being manipulated to employ a strategy or system that is not a good fit for the situation. Also, there is a good chance that some people have been a part of such an activity in the past and may be bored or disengaged as a result.

When you develop questions, discussion topics, surprise interventions, and audience involvement from scratch, you stand a better chance of engaging people. You also bring the wonderful element of surprise to the meeting or event. Remember, audiences today have a sense that they have "heard it all" and you will want to bring freshness to your work with them, especially freshness that is designed for them specifically.

Kevin worked with a group where his preparation centered more on who they were than on what he, the facilitator, would do or say. He prepped by finding out about them, interviewing them in advance, seeking their greatest challenges and their burning questions. When the group met, he formed them in a circle and had them re-identify these challenges, then sent them off into work groups of two or three for short periods of time to brainstorm ideas. Later the group constructed short role plays of situations they had previously discussed and worked on. Still later, in a large group circle format, they debriefed what they learned. Everything came from them, naturally. Kevin, of course, was fearless, on the outside!

Organic Facilitation Is Healthier in the Long Run

We know that many perceive organic foods to be healthier because they are grown with fewer pesticides and chemicals in carefully supervised growing conditions. The common tomato is a clear example; bright red, full tomatoes from your neighbor's garden carry more nutrients than the pinkish, waxy imports grown in a hothouse or far away on a commercial farm. Often, the result is we want to eat more of these better-tasting fruits!

Facilitating organically is healthier, too; when involvement occurs naturally and to the point, led by a skilled "farmer" with a watchful eye, the results are "tastier" and people come back for more.

At your next meeting, consider being the skilled farmer who tends to the others, watches them closely, perhaps even arranges them in specific ways. For a meeting with a small group, arrange them in a circle (yes, you can do this!) and begin the discussion at a point of their pain, what distresses them, challenges them, especially "lately," and what is of high concern for them.

Organic Facilitation Takes Time to Perfect (or, Actually, Make Appear Imperfect)

Less experienced presenters are often coached to use the tried-and-true activities and games to encourage interaction during what otherwise may have just been a speech. You, however, can be different. You can be immediately useful to your audience by:

- Soliciting "burning questions" (that is, what people most want to learn after their time with you today)

- Forming small groups to discuss or solve a problem and let them talk to one another

- Flip chart what they say and have them explain it to one another

- Asking your audience to apply the skills that they just learned

This is moving your audiences in a direction that will engage their astute listening and creative thinking on the spot, and it will not always come easily. It takes time and many imperfect attempts to discover the timing and appropriateness of the involvement.

Therefore, try beginning in some of the following ways:

- Acknowledge what few trainers allow themselves: it is OK, sometimes preferred, to be imperfect, to go with the flow, to "feel" your way.

- Know that your audience is there for the experience together and not only, or primarily, for the experience with you.

- Begin with a series of questions you ask rather than answers you have. Much of traditional training is about "giving" rather than about "probing," and in many ways traditional trainers omit the resource of the audience, the audience's innate brilliance and contributions.

- Give your content in targeted chunks or "lecturettes" of no more than eight to twelve minutes before you ask the audience to talk again with one another. If you are talking, or feel you need to talk, for forty-five to sixty minutes, know that you have lost them by minute thirteen. Yes, they will look like they are paying attention, but fear not, they are thinking elsewhere. And like some food, they will be hungry all too soon, having forgotten what went before.

- Outcomes are vital when you facilitate, as are burning questions. In fact, a good set of burning questions will give you an informal agenda for the meeting. Meet, address, or answer those questions and you will have one happy audience. The secret here is to gather the burning questions early on a flip chart, address them throughout the meeting, and then at the end of the meeting pull them out again and say to the audience one question at a time: "What did we say about this one?" Don't answer it yourself: have them do so. They know more about how it hit them, and it is a great way for you to discover even more about them—what outcomes they really received.

Intimacy Is Key

Say "presenting," and most people believe the job of the presenter is to get the audience to listen, take notes, and benefit from the wisdom of a speaker who stands behind a lectern facing them. What is really happening, however, is a most intimate one-to-one conversation with exactly one other person; in fact, when you speak to "everyone," you may be neglecting every one of them.

One of our students was a professional radio personality in Chicago. She had a nightly audience of just over 400,000 listeners. When we asked her, "How do you communicate with 400,000 listeners?" she replied, "Oh,

I don't do that. I only envision one person. I speak to one person all night long. That way every one of those 400,000 believes he or she is that one person!"

As you develop your notes for your next presentation, insert a reminder three or four times throughout to think about your audience as one person. It might even reduce your stage fright! Most importantly, it connects you to each audience member, who thinks, "Gosh! She's speaking to me!"

- You do this through your eye contact that is solid with each person.

- You will accomplish this by trusting the group itself when you allow them to speak in small groups, even rotating group to group: they meet more people, gain better ideas, and get to talk!

- You don't need to process or "report out" every conversation. Wait until the end of the session and have them summarize what they learned.

- Remember comedian, writer, and director Nora Dunn's advice, "Our job is not to please the audience; our job is to engage the audience."

As we "present," we want the other to have an open mind; we wish to establish credibility with this other person; and we hope to engage him or her in response—perhaps with a "yes" or perhaps with a question—often with applause! (We just have to be careful that the applause is not our first priority!) In order to enjoy the ambience of a one-to-one conversation, we need to first access the "inner listener" of the other.

On the now classic television series "Star Trek," a science fiction story about travelers in space seeking out new life and exploring where no one has gone before, the explorers were on a planet with a labyrinth of mines. As they explored, the crew and the miners were being harassed by a huge, deadly, and moving stone-like being. This eyeless, marking-free "thing" that looked like a huge boulder or mound was ravaging the miner community. This monster could cut through solid rock at a moment's notice. Miners were being killed; seemingly nothing could stop the carnage. The monstrous boulder seemed impervious to all weapons.

One of the crewmembers noticed there were also "little" boulders scattered all around the area, and they were moving! Finally, one of the crew, the half-human, half-Vulcan Dr. Spock, decided the huge mass needed to be addressed. He used an ancient Vulcan method, the Vulcan Mind-Meld. In it, he laid his hands on the huge stone, and then with great emotional and physical pain, energy transferred from the living boulder to Dr. Spock's awareness. Spock understood that this strange, deadly creature was pregnant! Like all moms, she was concerned for her "little ones" (who were being harvested by the miners!). Once understood, all came to terms. The miners realized she and her little ones could cut more tunnels faster and better than they could; the crew discovered a brand new being; and mom was happy to be understood and had her little ones in tow! Empathy existed even in outer space . . . one-to-one.

The best presenters do the same thing, one hopes with less pain!

Think about the stereotypical marital argument that you might see on late-night television. A wife spends hours preparing a home-cooked meal for her husband, only to be frustrated when he only says, "Thanks for dinner," before rushing out the door to play basketball. The husband buys his wife two dozen roses on the way home from work, only to be upset when she says, "My gosh! We don't have enough money for those flowers!" without recognizing his kind gesture. Gary Chapman coined the phrase "the five love languages," which refers to how people express heartfelt emotion. Some know they are loved when receiving gifts, some feel quality time with the other is the best feeling, some see love through physical touch, others recognize acts of service (like vacuuming) as the best display of love, and the final group of people only need to hear affirming words.

In this particular marital scenario, the wife believes her husband's love language to be acts of service, while he believes hers to be receiving gifts. Arguments flair up, Chapman says, because the love language we think our spouse has is not the language that our spouse actually has.

It's important in your presentations—just as it is in your most special relationship or marriage—to first "listen" in the language of the audience.

When you know that your spouse's love language is receiving gifts, you know that, while words of affirmation or acts of service are sweet gestures, it will be the gift that speaks the loudest. When you know that your audience most wants to know how you have outsold your nearest competitor two-to-one, you realize that your childhood memories of science experiments in the backyard may not be the most resounding to the audience members' ears.

The first access point to the audience is really a conversation during which the listener and the speaker share a special connection. A problem develops when we focus so closely on ourselves that, like the space travelers and the hypothetical marital argument, we only see boulders instead of potential partners, wasted money instead of a partner's display of affection through a gift. We don't understand what is really going on in the mind of the other. So when we don't understand the mindset of the audience during a presentation, we are left to focus on our message rather than on the meaning of the message for the other. The audience will remember the meaning of the message more than the message itself.

Understanding this part of a presentation leads you to recognize that your audience members want to talk, too! They want you to "know them" and they want to "be known." When you open up—not with a one-way monologue but with a dialogue that produces engagement, learning, and partnership—you build connections.

Fearless facilitators are always thinking audience, audience, audience . . . even if, or when, there is only one other to talk with you. This dialogue can never be processed or artificial. Fearless facilitation must be organic and bred in a free-range environment.

We recently saw a presenter who, for an entire hour, thought he was engaging the audience by finishing every sentence with one of the following questions:

- "Am I right or am I right? Let me hear you!"

- "Let me hear you say 'yes'!" (To which the audience dutifully responded, for a short while.)

- "So, we are talking about _____" (Again, he expected the audience to fill in the prescribed answer.)

This not only became predictable, tiring, and boring, but it also started from a false premise. He thought, and he said, that he was engaging the wisdom of Socrates (the ancient Greek philosopher and teacher who used questions as a way to engage students). He also thought, and he said, that this was an adult-learning model. In reality, it was far from it; it was instead a propaganda model. The audience had no opportunity to respond with their voice, for the "right" answer was that of the presenter's (one that he seemed to like a lot!).

Variations on this theme are abundant in sales meetings. You've been there: The presenter asks us to turn to the person next to us and say, "You are an amazing person and an amazing sales professional." or "Let's give each other a high-five and a standing ovation!" Or there is the motivational sales speaker we heard who peppered every few comments with the question "Agreed?" or the phrase, "Somebody help me here!" Finally, the audience became really, really quiet because they simply were tired of being coerced to contribute.

Fearless facilitators avoid the mistakes of these presenters who confuse repetition with learning, noise with engagement, and egocentric opinion with the real importance of the audience. Instead, there are several simple keys to encourage rather than discourage natural involvement:

- Really, really listen to them and then paraphrase what you heard; then ask the audience for their input;

- Make sure you are not a contributor, yet;

- Engage as many as you can "with" one another . . . avoid the traditional format of individuals talking from the large group to you;

- Put them in groups of two or three, maybe four, to let them discuss.

We promise you this will work! The differences among presenters are outlined in the chart below.

Traditional Presenter	Traditional Trainer	Fearless Facilitator
Content is king	Trainer process rules	Audience!
Lecture	Games	Discussion
Large group	Teams	Small groups
Applause	Thanks	Engagement
PowerPoint	Manipulatives	Flip charts
Solo prep	Committee	Audience

Contrast all of this with a presenter who is focused on the audience and who gives them a chance to talk to one another and express what they want to express (rather than what the presenter wants them to say).

An audience-focused presenter offers the audience time to ask any question, whether clarifying or discussion-provoking. We have all seen the frustration audiences feel when the presenter pauses and says, "Wow, we only have a couple of minutes left. Let's see if we have any questions."

The success-minded presenter allows the audience to reflect on what they think, then allows them to discuss and to determine what happens next for them.

The fearless facilitator is so convinced that the audience has the answers that most of his or her prep time is thinking, asking the audience, and planning very short lecturettes based around that information—which, depending on how things go, may not even be used!

You can present and facilitate organically when you keep artificiality from infecting your audience's experience. Give them the experience they really came for. If they did not come for the experience of learning with you, then all they require is for you to e-mail them your PowerPoint file.

You are in charge of the audience experience. Your job is to set up the audience for their learning and for their response. The audience is in charge of telling you what their experience was, for they are the only ones who really know and can speak to that.

Coach's Comments

What is my role as a facilitator if I am not there to present and inform?

The word "education" comes from the Latin "educare," meaning "to draw forth from." It does not mean "to dump into"! For too many years, people have regarded talking as somehow akin to teaching, which should result in learning and bettering us. Instead, we should see that learning and improvement come from the audience's collective past experience and the presenter's twist on an idea.

You are there to present and inform, and you are there for an important third reason as well: you are there to create a learning environment. The community of learners is there to unite around your message and make something of it. Remember the last time you went to a comedy club and had a great time? When you left, did you have trouble retelling the stories and jokes for those who were not there? That is because you had a community formed around only the presentation, not the digestion of the material. You were there to be entertained, not transformed. That your last training session left you unable to explain what you learned does not mean you had a positive community experience! Training sessions should focus on digesting content into directly applicable skills going forward.

When we are called upon to present in business, we are there to transform, and the data is sometimes a means to that end. If data were the only goal, you could simply send a printed report. The fact is that you were invited to be the presenter because you know more than the data. Your job is to take the audience from here to there with you. Be careful not to succumb to the adulation of being merely a good presenter. Rather, become a great teacher. Be the one who moves us.

Is There Ever a Reason to Plant an Idea with Someone in the Audience?

Absolutely not! An organic milk producer would most likely not bottle non-organic milk in containers labeled "organic" to save a few dollars one month, because if he or she were caught, profits and credibility might never recover.

In the same way, your "planted" questions will be found out! And when that happens, the audience will assume many unfavorable things about you. We know a senior executive who once took acting lessons so that when she had to fire someone or a group, she could cry on cue! It worked for her, until it didn't, when the word spread like wildfire. Your reputation is the reason you should never plant a question or comment with an audience member.

Fearless facilitation means you have to trust yourself and trust your audience. The simplest way to prompt them to talk to you is to encourage them to talk to one another. Faced with a fellow audience member, few can hide, and not too many can remain silent! Give them a chance to speak with one another. This is similar to a gourmet meal where you enjoy a chance to savor the food, the wine, and the company without racing to finish.

Simply say, "I want to give you an opportunity to respond to this material in a way that helps us all learn. When I give you the signal, please stand and find one other person who is not next to you and go and sit with him or her." After everyone is settled, say, "Please take three minutes and share what you think about _____." After some time, ask, "Tell me, what did you just learn from your partner?" Please, for everyone's sake, don't ask for reports from each group! When you ask them to learn, you are further engaging their creative thinking skills, deepening your lasting meaning.

How Do You Know When to Present and When to Facilitate?

While it might seem logical to present first and facilitate second, this may not always be the case. In some situations, consider a survey of the audience for their "burning questions," "hot topics," or even the agenda they wish the meeting would follow.

Some sales professionals do this when they ask us questions that help them find out what we need and want, what our level of expertise is, and how soon we want to buy. You can easily facilitate throughout your presentation by putting the audience in small groups of two or three to discuss ideas, develop alternatives, and determine next steps. Allow your presentations to be working collaborations as much as possible.

One word of warning, however: once you begin to do this, once you see what your audience experiences, and once they experience it, you and they will never go back to you being the only show in the room.

And your evaluations will soar!

Is There Risk to Facilitating Because Your Audience May Take the Conversation in a New Direction?

Yes, there is always that possibility. We actually titled this book *Fearless Facilitation* because of this risk, which is well worth taking. Some audiences are way ahead of us in their responses, in their thinking, and in their understanding. We want these audiences to have a forum to talk and, perhaps, even to lead. In this instance, we become transformative by helping the conversation flow. You don't need to be an expert in all content, only the alert expert facilitator, to help aid the learning flow.

There are also times when you might feel the content, the meeting, and even your presentation were hijacked. The meeting goes in an entirely unproductive way, off target, perhaps taken over by an audience member. No need to panic. Remember: you are in charge of your meeting, and if you are the designated presenter, it is your meeting! You have every right to say, "I want to jump in here and keep us on target and on schedule." Then find a connection between what is being said and what you want them to talk about: "It seems we've moved ahead of the new customer service initiative, and it's my job to remind us that we first need to decide _____."

If you have an audience member who strongly dominates, then do the same, saying something like, "Jack, I want to thank you for your question about the delivery piece and if it is OK with you, I'd like to put that up on the flip chart for now. We can return to it a bit later when we finish _____." Then go up to the flip chart and write

"Parking Lot" across the top with Jack's question beneath it as clearly and as succinctly as you can. Now, don't look at Jack (he'll start talking again!) and go back to your agenda. "Parking Lot" to Jack means this will be talked about later. "Parking Lot" to you means "Uhh, maybe!" In fact, at the next break go up to Jack and answer his concern one-on-one. It is unlikely he'll bring it up again.

How Can I Prepare to Facilitate?

Remember when you first started presenting? It was customary to have a well-rehearsed transcript of content in your head. You then perhaps gradually moved to note cards, and finally more "off-the-cuff." So, too, goes the progression for facilitating. Don't expect to do this seamlessly from the beginning. Being patient with yourself and your skill development is a key ingredient to becoming fearless.

Take a look at your presentation. Where are the natural places where the audience would benefit from time to think, to chew, and to digest your material? When do you want to find out what they think? What is a natural stopover during your presentation that would allow for talk and discussion? The caution here is that just because you want them to talk doesn't mean they know how. Remember that they have been trained their whole lives to sit and listen!

Don't be surprised if simply asking them what they think brings blank stares! Worse, it will only stimulate the opinion leaders and the extroverts. Don't do that! Instead, encourage them to talk with one another in small groups. Frankly, this one technique scares presenters the most. Do it just one time, and you will be cured of the fear that they won't get up and move. Even physicians, engineers, and high school coaches (the most hardened of audiences!) will do exactly what you tell them to do, as long as you look like you mean it. So make sure you at least look like you mean it! What scares us the most is asking a question of the audience. That is often known as "the great silence."

Three

The Fourth Wall

"The way I seek feedback is by way of my musical background. . . . As a drummer I have to be very aware beyond my set of drums. When I'm playing jazz, I am aware of everyone else; when playing rock, I am laying down the beat; with the symphony, I'm paying attention to the score and the conductor. So, in my work, I work to be very aware of what others are doing. . . . Respect is primary; no one opinion should take over, I can throw in my opinion, and mostly I am aware, seeking to understand. I guess in music and work trust is the basis."

—*Bryan Silbermann, CAE, President and CEO, Produce Marketing Association*

- Borrow from the theatrical to boost your connection.
- Break the wall and work the room to elicit audience wisdom.

Audiences don't like to be manipulated or forced to contribute (but they do want to be involved).

The Wall It's OK to Break

Actors learn about the "fourth wall" in Acting 101 classes; it is the invisible wall that separates the actor's world from that of the audience—the imaginary boundary between a fictional work and its receiver. Once the actor speaks directly to the audience through this imaginary wall, he or she is "breaking the fourth wall," and the boundaries are deconstructed. An example of this occurs in the classic Thornton Wilder play, "Our Town," in which the narrator steps out to the very edge of the stage. For a few moments, he is not representing a character; rather, he is just another person giving us a quick synopsis. He then backs away, again becomes a character in a fictional reality, and "fourth wall" is imagined again and "Our Town" comes to life.

We as facilitators and speakers also set up a "fourth wall" between ourselves and our content (far from fiction!) and our audience. Once we are up in front, we still set up a boundary between "us" and "them." The sooner we break the boundary by involving them in some way, the sooner we connect and involve.

This is why the traditional hour speech is not really so convincing or useful for today's audiences. Even politicians have begun to adopt the 'town hall' approach to indicate that they are more accessible to the electorate. While this isn't the most successful form of facilitation, for it is more of an intimate Q&A, it is a start to understanding that the "speech format" is less useful than in the past.

When presenters don't break the fourth wall, the audience observes the content. The fearless facilitator takes a step (pardon the pun) forward, breaking the fourth wall, so that the audience is focused on applying and connecting with the content.

Food, Fun, and Safety

When Cyndi's Labrador retriever, Max Maxey, was a puppy, she enrolled him in puppy training class. She insisted her teens attend and so the whole Maxey family arrived for the first class with little Max. The scene was adorable: twelve puppies on teensy leashes held by either first-time or inexperienced puppy owners. When the lively trainer walked in, she immediately engaged the participants in questions like, "For how many of you is this your first dog?" and "How many of you believe dogs either like or don't like you?"

"Well," she said, "I'd like to simplify things for you. Your puppy really only has three things on its mind at all times," and she walked over to the board and wrote the word, "food," saying "Is there food involved?" She next added the word "fun" and said, "Is this going to be fun?" Last, she added "safety," finishing with "Do I feel safe?" "Food, fun, and safety," that's all your puppy generally has in mind.

The puppy class trainer easily removed the "fourth wall" between herself and the rather anxious new "parents" by asking simple hand-raising questions followed by a perfect trilogy of easy-to-remember tips. From that point on, questions were exchanged easily, and the interactive tone continued for the rest of the eight classes. Of course, having a live animal or pet can almost always break down boundaries and barriers. There is an old theatre adage that advises not being upstaged by pets or children! Pets and children don't think twice about impromptu exchange and adaptation. Perhaps we should take our pets and children with us to every meeting! Chances are we would be more spontaneous.

Participants in our meetings ask the same questions as our pets. Is there food involved? Is this going to be fun (or at least something interesting, perhaps inspirational)? Do I feel safe (both physically and psychologically)? Through her technique, the puppy class facilitator answered these questions for us. She engaged us by providing nourishment, fun, and safety. We knew immediately that this would be a nonthreatening experience for us and for our puppies.

Three Keys to Providing Food, Fun, and Safety at Your Next Meeting

Through their expertise, understanding the audience's mindset, providing an enduring experience for the attendees, fearless facilitators provide food, fun, and safety.

Be an Expert. Know that you know what they want to know, regardless of their professional degrees or status in the organization. They came to this meeting to hear what you know; otherwise, they would have stayed away. From a full-blown presentation to a ten-minute update, you are important to them. They are also important to one another and this mix of you and them creates the ultimate learning experience for them. The puppy class facilitator introduced herself with a mini-biography that shared her experience training dolphins and other animals at the zoo as well as working for some time with dogs. So Cyndi's family and the rest of the group knew that they were learning from an expert.

Understand the Audience Mindset. How you convey your message will determine the effectiveness of your message. This means that you have to learn what is useful for them. This is why the puppy class facilitator asked us right away whether this was our first dog. She knew that was on our minds and had to be "released." The leader of the orientation class in your organization has a "go-around" warm-up immediately to establish that everyone there is new in some way. It's always important to ask yourself, "What is tantamount on their minds at this moment?"

Provide an Experience. Many meetings are missing an experience where the audience gets a "feel" for the material in a way that allows them to draw their own applications to everyday work. (Kevin used to take notes at meetings about what was said, but now takes notes on how he'll use what was said tomorrow. Most attendees, though, won't do this unless you give them the opportunity.)

Here, as a fearless facilitator, you'll be taking a calculated risk. Providing an experience that will make a memory for them means that they will be involved in the making of the memory. This is more than a "great speech" or "a riveting performance." Often, those events produce a memory of the presenter. What we seek instead is a memory created by the audience.

Remember that time in class when you "got it" in a way that was uniquely yours? You may have understood economics in a completely new and satisfying way; you noticed you were fluent in Spanish; you saw the color blue in a painting as never before; or you simply and completely participated in the music, the dance, the discussion as never before. These are the experiential moments that the lecturer cannot see, does not see, and is unwilling to plan for and provide. The puppy class facilitator involved us in doling out treats, giving commands, and praising our puppies so that we would remember how to do it at home. This would not have happened had she just lectured.

Five Tools for Your Fearless Tool Bag

Making fearless choices is not so difficult when you have the following practical "tools" in your "tool bag." These tools help build a positive mental framework that stands up in a storm! Additionally, you will be well-equipped to engage and inspire others at all times.

- Always provide an opportunity for the audience to talk to one another in as much of a one-to-one format as possible.

- Tone and edit your content to allow them to share their ideas too. The day of the forty-five-minute lecture followed by "We have a few moments for questions" is and should be over. When you become attuned to what is important for audiences, you may begin to notice that they come, not for the content that can be delivered electronically, but to be with you and with one another.

- Open yourself to being vulnerable in the sense that you may not know everything that will happen, that the audience will help you "cook the stew," and that your content is only the beginning. There is a growing trend toward doodling ideas and drawing diagrams on whiteboards and writable surfaces when explaining concepts and brainstorming solutions. Attention is strengthened and ideas are generated more productively when everyone is involved visually.

- Develop a knack, an attitude, and a skill for asking questions rather than giving answers. Rely on phrases like, "Tell us more about that," "Can you give us an example?" "How's that working for you?" "Anyone else have a different idea?" When you begin to ask instead of just answer or pontificate, you'll find even more questions to help others illuminate, explore, and create their own experience.

- Trust your expertise in ways other than lecturing. You appear much more confident when you plant the seeds one by one rather than dumping out the whole bag of knowledge at one time in a lecture. The seeds sprout much more successfully one at a time.

Three Rules for Breaking the Wall

We suggest breaking the fourth wall in every presentation you give. Once you experience the benefits: engaged audiences, a warmer ambiance in the room, and better reviews, you will want to continue. Here are three rules to follow for success:

- *Don't wait too long.* After your opening story or purpose statement is a good time to encourage involvement.

- *Ask specific, nonthreatening questions.* These questions don't have to be brilliantly difficult: in fact, the simpler the better. For example, "On a scale of 1 to 10, how do you feel about this so far?" or "What are your experiences with the system in your area?" Be sure to control the first responses, for you want it to go on just long enough to establish that your delivery will include the listeners. Most will be relieved to know that they'll be involved, and they will also be relieved to know that you can easily control the discussion.

- *Pre-select volunteers for first comments if you need to.* This technique is widely used by professional speakers. During your mingling prior to the program, cue in a friendly audience member that you'll ask a question about the topic and would appreciate his or her initiative in responding to break the ice. You can also approach participants during small group break-out discussions. Walk around the room and, as you listen, ask those who are particularly on track if they would share their key points with the larger group.

  You can also not select ahead of time and have some rules that you announce to the group. For example, "When I ask a question I'd appreciate it if someone would answer!" This often gets a laugh and gives them direction for what you expect. You can also suggest that any answer to any question be less than seventy-five seconds long. This adds some fun and allows for more interaction. (This is also good advice for you, the facilitator, as well, since long-winded answers become quickly boring and add to audience unrest and disinterest.)

> The fearless facilitator really thinks about how, when, and why he or she will break the fourth wall.

Dance Naked! The Wisdom Is in the Room

We were discussing stress and time management with a group of insurance claim adjusters at their annual conference. A very kind, polite group, their discussions were typically measured and correct. To stimulate discussion we fielded the question, "What do you personally do to manage your stress that works every time?" Imagine our surprise when our first volunteer response from a trim and lively middle-aged woman was, "I dance naked in front of the mirror every morning." The laughter took a while to die down. Truly, this is an example of a priceless gem you may receive when you ask instead of tell.

Another time we were working with a high-level pharmaceutical group, and as part of Cyndi's opening story, she fielded the question, "Who has the most unusual pet?" Several volunteers answered with pets from chameleons to unusual birds. Then the vice president in the back raised her hand and said, "I have a husband of thirty years. Does that count?" The room erupted in laughter. How could we as presenters have topped that? When a high-level audience member contributes with humor, it is a gift indeed.

> The fearless facilitator views audience sharing and stories as treasures to be cherished.

How to Work (and Not Work) the Room

Motivational and sales speakers have often been maligned for manipulative, "stagey" techniques used to involve group members. And rightfully so; in fact, the techniques that bloomed in the 1960s—pacing the stage, constant "hand-raising" questions, using too-loud volume and too much emphasis—are still painfully evident today. For example, we recently heard a millionaire sales professional who used these very techniques. Granted, his Internet marketing business was successful, but we felt "ambushed" by his speaking style: "How many of you know what I mean? Raise Your Hand! How many of you have ever felt like you've failed? Raise your hand! And how often have you gotten back on your feet? Raise your hand! That's right! Higher! Don't be shy! And how many of you are happy you came today? Great! Here's why!!! You are gonna learn. . . ."

Yikes!

When we're in the audience with this type of speaker, we cringe and feel bad not only for everyone there but also for the reputation of the entire speaking profession. If there is a place for this style, it is not with us!

Genuine, fearless facilitation occurs when the presenter easily mingles among the audience.

Lisa Sasevich, an Internet marketing millionaire presenter, does a great job of working the room as she presents. Lisa leaves the platform and walks among the audience. She doesn't involve them immediately but just simply walks among them. Heads turn to follow her as she meanders among the tables. Even though she has many "quippy" marketing slogans, such as, "It's your time; get on your dime," her style is so natural that they, too, seem natural. As she is continually on the move, attention follows her until—like a camera panning a shot—she mounts the platform again.

Another millionaire and very good speaker, Randy Gage, simply sits on a stool in front of a large audience and talks. Before he begins, though, he asks for a volunteer in the audience who can hold a microphone to help with audience questions. This is not an uncommon practice at meetings, so he easily gets a volunteer. But Randy adds a new twist; he then gives the volunteer a list of thirteen questions that typically arise during his program. As he presents, he then calls on the volunteer to ask one of the thirteen questions from his seat using the microphone. This is a great technique to keep the presentation varied and cue in the presenter (Randy) as to important topics not to be missed. It gives the entire presentation a sense of interactivity for the audience, and it is a brilliant way for the speaker to proceed without notes or PowerPoint slides.

The fearless facilitator learns from the millionaire presenters: success is in equality of sharing.

How Fred Friedman Broke the Fourth Wall

Fred Friedman is a speaker with an admirable personality. A well-known advocate for mental health, his personal journey includes time as a practicing civil rights attorney, homeless person, and recovering mental health patient with physical challenges as well. He presents frequently to mental health support groups, and we saw him at a local meeting of the Depression and Bipolar Support Alliance of Greater Chicago.

The venue was stark and simple: a basement room in an old neighborhood bank building. Fred was at the front and, due to his physical ailment, was standing slightly bent over from the waist. There was a rickety podium with a corded microphone, and the group also provided a second microphone for him to hold. He valiantly began with the hand-held, but nonstop static interfered. He moved to the podium microphone, only to find that it was also fuzzy-sounding. Finally, he just moved, without any microphone, to the center of the room, where he addressed a diverse group of about twenty nurses, community members, and a handful of people who had been diagnosed with depression and bipolar disorder.

As he told his story, we strained to hear at times, but he tried very hard to incorporate his entire audience with his eyes, pausing often to gather his thoughts and his breath. It was a stellar example of breaking the fourth wall. Some interruptive questions came as he presented, and now and then one person who appeared mentally unstable would stand up and move around and then sit in another place. None of this fazed him. It was clear he was comfortable with this crowd and with his wisdom. He carefully designed his talk around three points. "First, anyone can get sick, and getting sick can have disastrous consequences," he said. "Second, anyone can get better. And third, it is your responsibility to make it better."

At the end of the presentation he answered questions with humility and gave firm advice based on his personal experiences maneuvering the mental health system throughout his life. Fred was an inspirational facilitator, not only for how expertly he worked through the technical difficulties, but also for his awareness of his widely diverse audience and his flexibility with the environment. He created the atmosphere needed for this audience.

The fearless facilitator overcomes personal and technical challenges to inspire others.

Coach's Comments

How can one break the fourth wall comfortably when we typically don't do this at our meetings?

It's easier than you may think. Look at your typical opening remarks (for example, reviewing the purpose of the meeting, thanking certain members of the team, citing a key success story) and ask a question as you conclude the opening remarks. Here are some examples:

- *Review the purpose of the meeting.* "Before I continue, I'd be interested to know what your initial questions are."

- *Thank team members.* "Before I continue, I'd like to hear from the team. What made this project so successful in your eyes?"

- *Cite a key success story.* "How many of you have had a similar success recently? What happened?"

This method is nonthreatening to a group who may not be accustomed to being involved.

How can you "break the fourth wall" when leading a teleconference meeting?

- Try using the opening moments to "warm up" the crowd as they announce themselves online. You usually know who will attend; be prepared with specific comments that fit them, such as, "Joe, how did your presentation go?" or "Kevin, I noticed that your tenth anniversary with us was last week. Congrats!" You can also ask questions that directly tie into the topic, such as, "Sara, I'm looking forward to hearing your team's feedback on the budget."

- Remember to stand up when you are leading a teleconference; your voice will sound stronger, especially helpful for female facilitators, and you will be more aware (which is always a good thing!).

- Note the modulation of your voice. Put more expression into your voice on the phone so that the emotion registers. Sign language interpreters use not only their hands and fingers, but their eyebrows and expressions. This is done to create modulation, tonality, and emotion. Even though the deaf cannot hear, they can see the display and therefore are helped not only with the words but also the emotion.

- Be careful not to make it all about you. The best teleconference is like a "real" in-person discussion with interaction being shared.

Four

Have Fun with One or with One Hundred

"Be in alignment . . . ask what they need . . . demonstrate your expertise . . . be understanding about their needs and in the end make sure that you connect the dots for all of your stakeholders."

—*Bob Gilbert, President, MedStar Ambulatory Services, Columbia, Maryland*

- Yes, have fun! Actually, fearless facilitators have a great deal of fun because the fun comes from unpredictability, spontaneity, and just plain audience fun!

- Use the experts in the audience; utilizing their expertise to achieve more than only you could do before. Fearless facilitators know that the audience knows lots more than they do . . . and that is very OK.

- In an inclusive environment, you will produce results unheard of in ordinary meetings. Fearless facilitators know that an engaged audience is a working one; a listening-only audience may be listening to someone else . . . themselves!

Kevin experienced a "far from fun" audience recently. They were nice people: respectful, seemingly engaged, and cooperative. But they were just not very . . . fun! Where other audiences would laugh, this one politely smiled. Where others would nod and react, this one politely smiled. And where others would engage emotionally—yes, you guessed it—politeness ruled the show. And this was going to be a two-day seminar!

Every audience is completely different, even when we are (or think we are) exactly the same. Our job is to respect the differences and adapt. While some groups are quick and fun, others will be more laid back, intolerant, combative, or in need of resuscitation!

So What to Do?

- First, we have to listen intently when things are different than we thought they were or different from how we want them to be. Some cultures of audiences, both ethnically and occupationally, are a bit inhibited.

- Second, when their style is inhibiting you, go with what you planned and with just a touch more energy on your part. Don't wait for them to inspire you. Take the risk to be more effusive. More times than not, they will follow emotion; they will not follow hesitancy.

- Third, as you work harder, keep them moving around in small groups for discussion, flip-chart work, scenario role plays, etc. Nothing restores, or initiates, energy to a room as much as when the audience is involved in telling their own stories.

- Summarize frequently, but have them do it. In groups of twenty or fewer, circle them up from time to time (ignore any "Kumbuyah" comments!) and pitch a question to them that is vague and at least at a 40,000-foot level. ("So what is happening for you here?" or "What are you learning?" or "Let me open this up for you to say anything you want to say.") The secret here is to then shut up and wait for them to talk. No matter how long it takes, someone will pop. Resist the temptation to talk. Instead, use your hand to motion to the group non-verbally that they can respond. Usually you will be off to the races! Just be very, very careful to stay quiet. When you talk, they don't have to.

- Last, know for certain that this is what they need. They don't need your signature story, a joke, a nervous laugh, or even a game. They need you to be fearless!

Take It Professionally, Not Personally

As the presenter, be careful not to take any of this too personally. Instead, handle it professionally. Adapt quickly, seamlessly, and for the benefit of the audience. Here are some ways to do that:

Prepare by Learning About the Audience on a Personal Level and in Advance

Kevin often sends e-mails two weeks prior to his presentations and solicits answers to three questions from each member of the group. Their replies give Kevin a sense of the group and their challenges. Note this is different from sending a mass e-mail from a site like SurveyMonkey. Obtaining information is the secondary goal of these e-mails; the primary goal is connection through a personalized note. Web surveys are just the opposite.

Arrive at the Site Early and Greet Every Person, Again Personally

Once you begin your presentation, you will have friends in the audience and they will think, "I know that presenter!"

As You Take the Stage, Rely on Your Preparation and Experience

The last thing you want to do is wander through your presentation trying to obtain approval from the audience. They may already approve, even though they haven't informed their facial muscles yet!

Kevin was in the far-right box watching a musical that featured Mickey Rooney, a perennial and older song-and-dance man. Even at his advanced age, he was about to make his entrance. Those in Kevin's box had a view the rest of the audience did not: that of the wings just off stage. As the rousing music began, Kevin spied Mickey Rooney energetically, rhythmically moving his arms. Right on cue, he launched himself on stage like a twenty-year-old. Bang! He had made his entrance! He didn't wait for the audience; rather, he led them.

Advice to Preachers

You gotta read your self full,
think yourself ready,
pray yourself hot,
and let yourself go!

—Anonymous

As You Begin, Notice Who Is "with" You Through Their Reactions, Eye Contact, or What Seems to Be Working, Even in a Small Way

Fearless facilitators are on "high alert" in terms of their awareness from the first moments of meeting their audience members. Like ballroom dancers, they look for subtle signs of the "lead" and the "follow" and take steps to continue the "dance" through subtle and obvious signals. Fred Astaire, the famous dancer and actor, received many accolades for his dancing. His long-time partner, Ginger Rogers, once remarked that she did everything he did, just backwards and in high heels! The same goes for facilitators and the audience. When you observe them, it is much the same. It is never the facilitator "doing" something to the audience, rather they are "moving together" in all ways.

One way to sensitize yourself to these subtle clues is to engage your audience one person at a time as often as you can. We've recommended that you meet, greet, shake hands with, and speak to each audience member as he or she enters the room. You might also be aware as the meeting is underway who seems especially responsive to you and to others.

Kevin often refers to a room on the South Korean/North Korean border where diplomats meet. As he mentions this room, he is also scanning the audience for recognition signals about this room. When he sees it he grabs the moment and asks, "Have you been in that room?" Military or former military often have been. Kevin then turns the microphone over to them to tell their stories.

Kevin also finds a way to ask, "Who here is an Eagle Scout?" There is always a smattering of these former scouts who have achieved the highest honor in scouting. Once recognized, these audience members have a new status.

Audience members sometimes will volunteer funny or just plain interesting things about themselves . . . former Olympians, athletes who "went to state" in high school, those learning how to swing on a trapeze, Rubik's cube fanatics, fly fishers, and a host of others.

Fearless Facilitators Are Always Aware of Who Is and Who Could Be in the Audience

At these times especially, notice what you are doing that might be helping this interaction:

- Are they more connected with you when you depart from your PowerPoint slides? (Yes, they often are!)

- Are they slightly more responsive as you move physically closer to them? (Almost always!)

- Are they busily taking notes? (Maybe you said something of high interest!)

- Are you too quiet? (A stronger, non-obnoxious volume will bring more attention and credibility.)

- Do they need to be reassured? (That any answer is OK.)

- Have they been introduced to one another? (Do this early and often.)

- Do they need some refreshments? (Sure!)

While you don't want to come across as a know-it-all, you need to bring what we call your "stage ego" to the forefront. It is never good to be egocentric in an obnoxious way, but it is certainly OK, often necessary, to bring your ego, your sense of self, and your confidence to the stage, to this audience.

Kevin speaks to many physicians who can be both a wonderful and a judgmental audience. He has learned that teaching doctors is truly "herding cats". . . big ones! (Lions, Tigers, and Bears!) And just as you would when confronting them in the wild, you make yourself look big, you show no fear, and you step forward into the audience when you speak. Like many professional audiences, they respect this outer self-confidence, even if you don't feel it on the inside!

Cyndi will often "wade into" the audience, as a good teacher often does. She's never behind the lectern or podium and moves throughout the room, not worrying about audience members who have to turn their heads to keep up with her. This makes her available to the audience, more intimacy is developed, and it gives her critical access to them. Moving allows her to read their body language, non-verbal cues, and side comments alike.

This Is Your Meeting, Your Time, Your Moment, and the Audience Is Depending on You to Make It Happen

So muster up your courage and recognize that audiences are different and are in need of our next right step with them. Often, acting as if you are in charge is just enough, even though you may feel far from it!

This is an important component of facilitation, acting as if, because it allows you to create what might not yet be apparent:

- The audience isn't digging you? How would you be if you acted as if you knew that they silently were loving you? (This, by the way, is often the case. Don't judge yourself based on their bland facial expressions—they could be thinking!)

- You have a hostile audience? That's OK because you can act as if they are not hostile, simply forthright and putting things out on the table!

- Do they seem bored, disinterested, perhaps distracted? Simply act as if they really are! Put them into small groups of two or three with a focus question, and we promise you, the energy in the room will rise exponentially!

- Mostly act as if you are the one to help them interact, to create a learning community, to help them achieve the goal. Act as if, and it will happen!

Once, with an unruly but nice crowd, Kevin found himself saying, "Usually I don't lose control of the audience this quickly!" They laughed (though Kevin was dead serious) and in a strange way they seemed to feel "known." He still doesn't know whether they changed or if it helped that he declared "presenter bankruptcy," but in any event, things improved. Did they really improve or did they act "as if" they changed? Kevin didn't care!

Be Ready to Adapt

While your boss may have brought you in to give the same presentation that you've given several times before, always be ready to adapt. This is not easy to explain or to do, but when you are willing to adapt, you often gain just enough momentum to find yourself doing the right thing (whatever that is!) to make a difference. The real advice here is to avoid being rigid, predictable, upset, or even angry with your audience. You will come across as that legendary evil elementary school teacher that all of us had at one time whom we still resent! In these situations, few root for the teacher!

Adapting means:

- Listening to the dissenters a bit more closely than to those who are loving you up.

- Being willing to drop some slides or content that seem not to fit now that you have this particular audience in front of you.

- Taking a break a bit earlier, allowing for some quiet time for them to reflect as if they were on a retreat, or even reflecting with them on how things are going.

- Adapting can also mean using the moment to engage them. Consider the military technique of the "hot wash," which is a fast and structured way to debrief after an event. Simply draw a line down the middle of a flip-chart sheet and ask, "What did we do right here? What do we need to do better next time?" This is a remarkably simple time-tested technique for group self-reflection. Again, we guarantee it! (As do the USAF, US Army, etc.)

Open your ears to what they want and to what they are expressing. Give them an opportunity (early and often!) to talk to each other, even in short three-minute snippets. Listen well to what they say to one another and to the large group. In the same way we know our adolescents best when we shut up and listen, sometimes it works with audiences, too! In fact, it always works with both!

Look at and talk to individuals when you see a chance to personally engage them. Take part in short conversations, questions, and encouragement as they move around in small groups. The fearless facilitator walks up to random groups, listens in, and nods approvingly. At coffee breaks, continue the conversations and be inquisitive. Be sure to approach those who seem the most disinterested, most apart, and even the most disapproving of you. You will be amazed at what this one technique can do for the life of your audience.

Remember that someone in your audience is distracted with the divorce he was just asked for, the migraine she is trying to ward off, a child who is ill, even someone who is on the verge of quitting his or her job. We will never know much of these expressions, but it helps to know they could be present. Sometimes when we are seen as engaging, we will be seen as safe enough for them to engage us with whatever they want to tell us.

While you are the expert and the presenter, remember that your audience is really full of "value interpreters." They are the ultimate arbiters of your value. Increasingly, they value the experience, not just the data or the lecture . . . no matter how important the presenter is or thinks the data is! Every business has to show value compared to its price. Why would someone pay $500 per night at one hotel rather than $100 at another hotel in the same city, same street, and same area if all he or she was going to do was sleep? It is because the sleeper values what one has over the other. Perhaps this is prestige, or a feeling of safety, or the promise of more comfort, attention, and specialness. Or perhaps someone else is paying for it!

The fact is that the same value resides less in the thing and more in our understanding of what the thing does for us, to us, and with us. So, too, with your presentation, teaching, or facilitation. The audience has a conundrum that they want solved. How well you are perceived as being able to solve it will determine your value to them.

Know That You Can't Win Them All

While you can be an excellent presenter every time, you must accept that some presentations are better, more fun, and more memorable for you and the audience than others.

The presentation experience, while being a group experience, is also a deeply personal one. You will undoubtedly receive many A+ grades, but don't feel that you need to score at that level every time. Similarly, your audiences don't have to be graded the same way by you each time. Fearless facilitators judge themselves and others by a newer standard: "Was I useful to them?" This new standard helps with deliverables and is outcome-focused.

You can help your audience become more effective by helping them tap that inner courage of theirs to take the next right step in their development. However, if you don't permit yourself to think big about this outcome, you may instead settle for a more transactional effect.

You can be of great use to the person calling the meeting by helping him or her deliver the message. When you know what this person wants the audience to know, feel, and do as a result of the meeting, you can focus in a laser-like way and better produce useful results. If, however, you distract yourself by seeking approval or being evaluated as great, you may become hopelessly sidetracked.

- You can be of tremendous help to yourself by not burdening yourself with the demand to be perfect or flawless.

- Trust the collective wisdom that exists in the audience. Remember that when you are stuck or someone asks a tough question, there is wisdom in the group. Those people have come together because you are there. It was the *Star Wars* movie that popularized, "Trust the force, Luke!" What was really being said was "Trust yourself, Luke!" When you are unsure, trust the force you have inside of you. Then you can remember another famous quote from science fiction: "Live long and prosper."

Yes, Facilitation Works with Very Large Audiences!

You can use most of the same interactive techniques that you use with smaller groups with larger groups. The difference lies in three areas: how you set up directions, how you get out among the crowd, and how you manage the timing of the overall activity.

Give Extremely Precise Directions to Large Crowds

Larger crowds need a very clear and deliberate set-up for anything you will be asking them to do. Even locating a pen and paper can take a while. Even with very smart attendees, when we say, "You'll need paper and a pen for this next activity," adults are scrambling for pens. This may seem odd, but it happens and it will curtail your flow, distract them, and waste time. The solution? Have a basket of pens ready! To set up for success, before you even begin the activity, alert them that you would like to engage them in a brief activity. Then, slowly and clearly, explain exactly what you would like them to do.

For example, you might say, "Let's do something a little different. When I count to three, please put down all of your materials, stand up, and silently find another person who is not sitting next to you and have a seat." Large groups will tend to stall, giggle, laugh, converse lightly, or simply not hear the directions, so a clear set-up helps them focus. (Make sure you can be heard, as well. Cyndi once set up a large group activity for a group of two hundred attendees, unaware that the speakers in the back of the room were not turned on. So while those in the front of the room complied, the audience in the back of the room was confused.) Quickly and without a sweat, she moved to the center of the room and pointing to the front of the room said, "Do what they are doing with somebody!" (Remember, fearless facilitators don't worry about being perfect!)

Monitor the Large Crowd by Becoming Part of Them!

While getting out and among the audience is always important for the large-group facilitator, it is especially important once you allow them to break into groups and "do their own thing." As this occurs, leave the stage or front area. Wander the room throughout the activity, returning to the front only to give timing cues or to review directions. As you mingle, remember our fearless facilitation mantra: listen and comment with encouragement. We may not be able to say this enough: you have to be an encouraging presence to your group of learners. Get a sense of what they are most focused on and whether they understand the discussion goals. If you sense something amiss, quickly correct it.

In the largest of venues, something as simple as the presenter stepping off the stage, wandering through the audience, speaking with eye contact, and being fully and physically present to the most is the simplest form of encouraging audience intimacy. Once back on the stage, the next logical step is to ask them to form new small groups. Each new group, each new focus question for them is not repetition, it is depth.

Large Groups Consistently Need More Time for Even the Simplest Tasks!

A third area of attention for the large-group facilitator is how to monitor timing. Usually, it will take just a bit longer due to crowd control—getting people focused and winding people down. While you can take as much time as you want with an interactive activity in the confines of a large room, you do want to keep aware of your timing, whatever the topic and learning objective. It can be as brief as a three-minute exchange (we love these) or as long as fifteen to twenty minutes. The point is to monitor the energy, the pace, and the learning. It is not vital that you unpack every small group exercise; in fact, simply moving them from group to group is energizing for them.

Often, we ask audiences to find partners. In larger groups, we then ask the partners to join another partnership to discuss in a group of four, then ask the group of four to join another group of four so that a small group of eight is formed for a discussion. The large group becomes a lively room full of groups of eight, all getting to know each other and some key thoughts on the topic. This is a wildly successful and nonthreatening way for people to mingle. It is also a nice break from sitting in an auditorium or in classroom-style seating all day.

Adapting to an Unexpectedly Small Audience

A colleague shared a mental mantra she uses when the crowd is unexpectedly small. She tells herself, "The right people are here; the right people are in the room." What a positive approach for those times when only a few show up! This has certainly happened to us; in fact, we've even facilitated a session with one attendee!

The fearless facilitator never, ever complains about the small turnout and instead "cheerleads" for the great information he or she has and the opportunity to discuss it . . . with the "right" people!

Provide Personal Attention

If only one person attends a meeting, this provides a natural setting for personal attention, lots of questions, or even coaching, depending on the situation. You can still present your key PowerPoint slides, if data is important, adding interaction around each one, such as, "How do you feel about these results?" or "Is this what you expected?" If the situation suggests one-on-one coaching on the topic, ask the sole attendee if that is what he or she prefers. Then get a sense of the issue with which you can help him or her. If there are several people present, begin with their burning questions and adapt your presentation accordingly.

Kevin once had five doctors in a two-day seminar that was supposed to have sixty-five in attendance. There is no way they would put up with a two-day lecture, even if Kevin could have mustered up the courage, content, and competence to do so! With lecturettes, discussion, Q&A, and interviews of one another . . . the meeting could have happily gone on for a week.

This meeting would have been productive for an entire week for the same reason that engagement; connection, and facilitation work so well with audiences. They want to contribute, to talk to one another, to explore, and to learn. For too many years, we have equated learning with content alone, asking the learner of any age to sit and take notes. We even hear presenters say, "Yes, I would love to have the audience ask questions and talk to one another, but I just have to plow through this content!"

You can plow all you want. Your value interpreters, however, will continue to suffer from wandering minds, distracted by meandering thoughts, silently judging you, and leaving with very little of what you really said.

Control the Environment

If you are able, arrange the seating so that you and your small group are in proximity. Get rid of extra chairs. Sit around one table. Form a circle of chairs down front in the auditorium. Open the windows. Dial up the lighting. Encourage and take advantage of a more intimate setting. It will promote a more intimate discussion. Anything you can do to remove obstacles will be richly rewarded. Kevin is at the point where he downright insists that there be no tables when he presents.

Coach's Comments

- What do groups of six and six hundred really have in common?

These groups have one thing in common: they want the experience that solo learning does not allow. Why do you attend a concert? It's about the group experience and the excitement that live entertainment provides. If you want the music, then go to iTunes; the concert is all about the group. Entertainers know from daily experience that every audience has its own personality. This is why it is never "just another show." Jon Bon Jovi is known for telling his band and crew before each show to play as if this is the last show of their lives. He understands what some professional speakers still do not: every audience's unique personality, the speaker's personality, and the manner in which content is explained is never the same twice.

- These techniques feel a bit "seat-of-the-pants" to me. Do I run a risk of losing control?

This depends on how you see yourself. If you see yourself as an impeccable presenter, a rock star, a famous celebrity, then losing control may be a big problem! On the other hand, if you see yourself as one who helps others by making things easier (like a teacher, a helper, or a facilitator), losing a little bit of control means you are focused on your audience. Being slightly out of control equals dynamic learning, not utter chaos! Consider the difference between reading about how to drive and actually being in the driver's seat beside your instructor. Or consider the difference between knowing about CPR and understanding how to use the technique to actually save a life. Or how about this—reading a book about facilitation and actually making it happen! Facilitation is cooperative conversation. Socrates began all of this in ancient Greece by asking questions instead of lecturing. The focus shifts to the audience so they can share questions, conclusions, experiences, and expertise with each other.

- Aren't I supposed to be the expert? I'm the presenter, after all.

You are the expert and so is your audience. Your content expertise is only part of your skill; your ability to teach, influence, and transform is the other part of your expertise. Remember those teachers you had who made a difference in your life? Remember the ones who thought they did?

- When do I as the presenter actually get to present?

Kevin likes to call the content portion "lecturettes," since they serve the purpose of content in bite-size portions with interactivity at each level. Think about your favorite restaurant experience. The food was important, but it wasn't the only important part. Chefs serve the dishes one at a time so the diners can chew, savor, and talk. You should as well. Lecture a bit, ask the audience to talk a bit, seek questions, and perhaps then ask the audience what they think is the answer. Then give your thoughts—or maybe, just maybe—listen and become a learner, too.

- What will experts say that will revolutionize the meeting?

Experts, authors, specialists, and researchers are vital to any meeting. What revolutionizes a meeting is the intangible experience, especially how fun it was for them. There is nothing frivolous about having fun any more than adding a bit of salt to ramp up the taste of a special dish. Too much salt (or fun) is a big problem; none at all can be pretty bland. But just the right pinch of salt and fun can transform a meeting and revolutionize the experience.

- How do I involve my audience when my boss wants just the employees to be there so he can talk at them?

It's OK; let him do that. Then you can put everyone into groups of three and ask them to discuss what they heard him say. In new groups of three, ask them what questions they have for him. Then, in one more group of three, ask the employees what they believe they will need to change to make his ideas a reality. Few bosses will object to that! Make it safe for him and for his agenda to be heard.

- Do these principles apply the same way to a small audience as they do for a large audience?

We have used these techniques in small and large venues. In the largest of venues, something as simple as the presenter stepping off the stage, wandering through the audience, speaking with eye contact, and occasionally placing his or her hand on the shoulder of an audience member is the simplest form of encouraging audience intimacy. Once back on the stage, the next logical step is to ask people to form small groups. Let them talk.

They do remember what they said and what their peers said. When you as the presenter/facilitator, the fearless facilitator, help them learn from you and from one another, they leave with more, much more.

Five

Dialogue Not Monologue (Worse, Duologue)

"The best moderator is the one an audience will stop directing questions to."

—Ken Johnson, Pharm.D., Executive Director, Corporate Medical Affairs,

Durata Therapeutics, Inc.

- The great facilitator is also a great conversationalist.

- Lively and enriching conversation is a learned skill.

- Dialogue is part of preparation, follow-up, and coffee breaks.

Conversation Is Not Easy for Most

Largely introverted, most of our population is not comfortable with small talk. Typically, 70 percent of the population has experienced shyness at some point. If this is your style and you want to be a fearless facilitator, we have three words for you: get over it! You will need to be the model for an easy conversation that results in dialogue as opposed to monologue.

Susan Cain, author of *Quiet: The Power of Introverts in a World That Can't Stop Talking*, makes a compelling case for how to be yourself and get over yourself in a world that may not value your quietness. (www.ted.com/ talks/lang/en/susan_cain_the_power_of_introverts.html)

Many professionals are not well trained in the art of conversation. Author Dale Carnegie discovered that need years ago with his best-selling book *How to Win Friends and Influence People*. Carnegie asserted that a smile, the ability to listen, to show interest, and the sincere desire to understand the other person's situation were instrumental in gaining influence. These behaviors apply both one-to-one and in group facilitation and leadership. Your audience will be enthralled at your ability to create and maintain a dialogue with them, whether spontaneously throughout or at selected points in the presentation.

Carnegie's book was written close to eight decades ago, and yet it is still a popular text for our classes of undergraduates! The stories they bring to class about their parents (and their grandparents!) having read and been "formed" by Carnegie's concepts is truly an unforgettable experience.

Carnegie's key concept of being truly interested in the other person is certainly a universally laudable goal, yet how many times do you see it violated with so many of us so very willing to go on and on and on about ourselves.

Once in an airport lounge, Kevin heard a man go on about his many skills: hiring wisely, knowing when to coach, how he was smart enough to arrange to see Neil Diamond on two different continents in the space of two weeks, and playing "ever increasingly superior golf." His colleagues, who were perhaps his employees, put up with this by skillfully exercising the best of Carnegie: making him feel as if they were interested. Perhaps they were. The rest of us could only admire their riveting skill!

The fearless facilitator is truly interested in the other person.

Can You Converse Without a Cocktail?

If you've ever attended a wedding where alcohol is consumed, then you know how much more freely conversation flows after guests have a couple of drinks. It is a sure sign of maturity if you can converse prior to the champagne toast. Try it! Of course, many cultures and religions prohibit alcohol, and there is most likely much to be learned from observing their conversational abilities. Rarely is alcohol served at a church service, and perhaps the coffee hour following the service is a perfect place to practice your conversation skills. In fact, Cyndi met one of our best editors at a church coffee hour and developed a lifelong professional relationship and friendship.

Be honest and assess your own ability to converse without a cocktail. If you admit to being much more conversant with one, then consider what you can still do without one. Simply make a comment or ask a question about the event or the other person.

- *Person:* (Referring to name tag) I notice your name is spelled like my grandmother's. How did you arrive at that? Is it a family name?
- *Event:* How often do you attend this conference?
- *Person:* How long have you been in sales? Did you start in a sales career?
- *Event:* So far today, what is your main takeaway from this session?

The Fearless Facilitator Accesses Conversation Topics About the Event or the Person

Our colleague in the National Speakers Association, Dr. Loren Ekroth, focuses on the art of conversation. Dr. Ekroth writes:

"Although talking with others is natural, in certain situations it takes courage to converse. Here are some common reasons for these fears and some ways to find the required courage.

1. *Appearing ignorant.* You may 'clam up' when talking to persons more knowledgeable than yourself because you don't want to reveal how little you know. One effective way to handle this is to admit not knowing and to be a learner willing to ask questions of the other(s). Management consultant Peter Drucker, wrote 'My greatest strength as a consultant is to be ignorant and ask a few questions.' You can be comfortable talking to very smart people if you are willing to learn from them.

2. *Touchy topics.* Some have called this concern as 'off-the-table-itis,' a social infection that prevents people from bringing up matters that might cause discomfort or conflict. One way to reduce your fears so you can talk about an avoided topic is to seek help from a trained counselor or mediator whose presence and skills provide safety. Another way is to agree upon a place and time to talk about an avoided topic with civility and privacy. This allows you time to reflect upon an issue and prepare your thoughts in advance of your talk.

3. *The rich, famous, powerful, beautiful, and handsome.* Many report feeling tongue-tied and afraid of saying something stupid. The hesitation almost always stems from self-consciousness, the preoccupation of how you will be seen by the 'special other.' If you take your focus off yourself ('How am I doing?') and put it on the other person, and if you think of this as a wonderful opportunity to talk with an unusual person, much of your awkwardness will melt away. Ultimately, conversation confidence rests upon skills. The greater your level of conversation skills, the more confident you'll be when talking to a variety of people in many different situations. The term for this is 'self-efficacy,' knowing you can do something because you've done it before."

From *Better Conversations* newsletter, April 4, 2012, by Dr. Loren Ekroth. © 2012. Reprinted with permission. Loren Ekroth is founder of "Better Conversation Week" and related community events. To subscribe to his complimentary newsletter, visit www.conversationmatters.com.

Conversation: Begin at the Beginning

The art of conversation for the facilitator begins in the preparation. A great facilitator interviews selected participants in advance of the program, meeting, or event. Phone conversations are best, and the opening of the conversation is an important place to set a nonthreatening conversation. With a friendly tone, and a focus totally on the other, the facilitator begins to get a sense of the future audience member. This conversation begins with light icebreakers such as, "How is your week going?" and " I'm intrigued by your name; is it Irish?" Then the phone interview moves to other questions such as, "Tell me what your goals are for this program" or "I'd be interested in knowing more about your experience with the IT department." The pre-meeting interview sets the tone and allows the participant who may not know you to gain a sense of your style and approachability.

The next important time for conversation and dialogue is as your audience enters the room, webinar, or teleconference. Again, your ability to converse sets the tone. Keep the focus off you and on the participants. Find the lightest of topics to break the ice: the weather, current events, sports, what the person is wearing, the seating arrangement, the room or event, or names and job roles. Do this with all levels; if the VP or CEO enters first (which is rare), don't be intimidated. Take the opportunity to establish yourself as someone he or she will enjoy having lead the meeting. We have discussed dogs, ice cream, architecture, what's on the wall, and more as we meet those who first enter the room. The place not to be is fiddling around with your laptop or projector, if you can arrive early enough to set both up. If you just cannot arrive in the room in time to do this, learn to converse as you manage your audiovisual equipment. It's a true art that can show immediately how professional and experienced you are in your role. All these early attempts to connect will pay off. You will be able to mention these conversations when appropriate and even refer to specific things you've learned by conversing with folks as they arrive.

The Break Is Never Really a Break

The great facilitator knows that the break is never a time for stuffing his or her mouth with the catered food and drink. Be last in line; serve yourself a small helping of the easy-to-eat options, and take small bites while meeting anyone you haven't yet met. Here the conversational focus can encompass the material you have been discussing, but try not to let it be totally on business. Find out more about the participants—their backgrounds, families, and work experiences. Compliment anyone who has been particularly involved; let the more difficult participants know that you appreciate their perspectives and ability to share them in the program or meeting.

Dialogue During Your Meeting

Keep in mind that most people are introverted and prefer to collect their thoughts before speaking. As you facilitate conversations, they will respond to your probes such as, "Tell me more" and "That's interesting; can you explain that a bit more?" They can also be encouraged to contribute by using their names and a reference to their expertise. For example, you may offer, "Susan, you have many years in the subscriber services area; what changes do you see as you develop subscriber relationships?"

One of the best ways to control the extroverts is with humor and a lighter touch. For example, you may say, "Joe, it's clear today that you're a fan of system upgrade. Let me get a sense of what others may think as well."

The more conversational and two-way you can keep your presentation, the more people will be able to remember. Keeping attention nowadays with smart phones and tablets out is more difficult than ever. Learn and use participants' names, move about the room, and ask frequent questions. When you appear to be more of the partner in learning than the superior lecturer, your outcome will reflect your skill.

Dialogue Post-Meeting

Don't give up on conversation just because your event is over. Follow up with immediate questions on how you did and what next steps will be. Most people will have to be reminded at least twice to respond because they are unaccustomed to seeing the importance of follow-up. It's good to send "thank-you's" to involved participants who helped move the discussion along by offering ideas. People tell us they don't receive enough encouragements at work—ever. You can be the one to help them with "What I really liked about what you said. . . ." "What I learned from you is. . . ." "What I appreciate is. . . ." You can use this throughout your work with them in the large group, small group, and especially in your one-on-one conversations.

In Sum, Five Steps for Fearless Conversation

1. Plan ahead for topics to discuss by interviewing or e-mailing those in attendance or those in charge.

2. Break the ice and converse as the audience enters the room.

3. Continue conversation during lunch and breaks.

4. Encourage introverts and control extroverts as needed during your meeting.

5. Post-meeting, continue the conversation with a few questions via web or e-mail.

Coach's Comments

- I dread going to the big conference we have every year. Are there any tips for the shy person who absolutely must attend and be seen and heard?

Consider pairing up with an outgoing personality. This person can introduce you and help you with the most difficult conversational step—breaking the ice. Be careful that you don't rely on this person for the entire event. You can also contact the meeting planner beforehand and gain a sense of how you can help or when certain mingling events really start. Most companies can use extra hands at the registration table or with any drawings or contests. If you can be in a role where you are doing something, you'll be more comfortable. Keep in mind that most people feel the same way you do and are probably delighted when you approach them with a conversational topic. At a conference, you can always talk about the speakers, the topics, the venue, and the hotel or travel. "What session did you attend today?" is typically a successful start. Try to keep your topics positive rather than negative, such as, "My hotel room is so small; how's yours?"

- How do I avoid an over-talker or too-strong personality during a meeting or event? How about when I am the speaker in front?

Much can be done non-verbally; as you valiantly attempt to end a conversation or interrupt in a mannerly way, the over-talker tries to keep you planted by planting his or her eyes or body in line with yours. Back away a bit, glance away, put your plate or drink between you and the talker, and slowly send the message that you would like to move away.

When you're the speaker, your move is similar; never let an over-talker "corral" you to be in his or her space and in eye contact for long. As you answer, move away and look at the other participants. When answering the question, look at the person as you answer, but end your answer by looking at someone else. Looking back at the person is the equivalent of giving him or her the microphone for yet another interaction.

In both cases, honesty is the best policy. During an event, say something like, "Interesting talking with you; I'd like to meet a couple other people, so maybe we'll see each other later." Another move is to involve other people in the group with you. Sometimes you will see someone alone, off by himself or herself, and you can say to the over-talker, "Let's go introduce ourselves to that person, I saw her earlier and wanted to say hello." This involves another person, which will allow you to make a graceful exit. Remember, you don't have to feel cornered, but you do want to be courteous. Many over-talkers are insecure and, while they don't understand the effect they are having, they are extremely sensitive to slights. So be careful that any exit you make is not abrupt. Make it natural; you can even excuse yourself to go to the washroom!

During a presentation, use your best facilitator controlling phrases such as, "Thank you for that perspective; I'd like to hear from some others and see what other perspectives are out here." The rest of the group is hoping you'll control the strong personality; they're with you as you remove yourself from the situation and move the conversation forward for the rest. If you are still plagued by the dominator, then use the flip chart to record his or her main points, keep involving others, add their ideas to the flip chart, and then say, "I have an idea. Move into groups of three. I have a question for you." Then once they are in groups, give them a focus question that in some way relates to the flip chart and in a bigger way to what you want to move to next.

Let's say the flip chart is full of the dominators' complaints about healthcare policy. Your triad topic would then be "What are three opportunities your group sees for rectifying the situation or getting things back on track and why." Move to a positive and they will follow.

When somebody enters Mehmood Khan's office, he always starts the conversation with a personal question and never a business question.

> "Here they are in the office of their boss or their boss's boss, one of the five senior executives of the company, I have to be sensitive to that. At least with a personal question there are no wrong answers!
>
> "Then, I like to let the conversation start where my subordinate informs and educates me, rather than the other way around. First, this gives him or her confidence, becoming my teacher. If I begin it can shut things down, especially if I begin with the 'why, how come' questions.
>
> "Second, this 'me as student, them as teacher strategy' can help me validate my assumptions. Once you have expressed an opinion, it is emotionally hard to move away from it. I also like to use 'approachable engagement' where everything is 'we,' especially when there is a disagreement or errors or an

issue. 'Guys, we haven't thought this through' is much better than 'You haven't done this or that.' The funny thing is now that their bosses are warning them, 'Hey, if Mehmood says he doesn't know, don't believe him!' Even this is good, because they come in and get to the point without too much detail.

"I do like to set up the question and then not answer it. You have to always size up your audience. They all come from different places, specialties, and backgrounds. The question creates the emotional pull early on."

—Mehmood Khan, MD, FACE; CEO, Global Nutrition
Group; SVP and chief Science Officer, PepsiCo

Six

The Set-Up

Making It Happen

"When facilitating my first group in a foreign country, I wasn't sure what to expect. However, my main goal was to keep them engaged. I condensed my wordy presentation to encourage group discussion and learned flexibility was key!"

—*Mirella Saucedo-Marquez, Vice President, Private Banking, Credit Suisse*

- Set up discussion topics and activities "gently" so people actually do them instead of complaining or going silent! You want to be careful not to make this look too much like games they may have played in the past or routine icebreakers or even team-building tactics.

- Recognize that setting up authentic interaction works one-to-one as well as with groups. Talking to your boss, preparing a vacation with your child, and even talking to your physician can all become important moments of interaction that depend on you to make them happen.

- Every member of your audience and team is a value interpreter. As such, they are the sole "experts" on your meeting skills, and they are the ones to take the message and do something with it . . . or not! Therefore, tuning ourselves into the audience pays big dividends for them and for us. We become useful by our relentless focus on them, not on their evaluations, but on them.

As we mentioned before, keep in mind that setting up a facilitation experience is a bit like a chef preparing the ingredients of a great meal or an artist preparing the surface before painting. How you begin, what you assemble, how you think about the finished product, and how you regard the recipients, will make or break your effort.

Our Facilitation Manifesto

- We believe it is more important for your audience to engage with one another early and often than it is for you to delay interactivity until you believe they have mastered what you are teaching.

- We believe the presenter is neither the most important person in the room, nor even the wisest one.

- We believe that audiences, like good ingredients, need to be mixed, simmered, added, and allowed to combine to produce the best results.

- We believe the job of the presenter is not to "present the data" but to "facilitate the learning" about the data.

The fearless facilitator understands that the audience is not there to be entertained by or to learn from the grand master at the podium. Rather, audience involvement is what will make the experience special for the whole group, and the collective wisdom of the group is what will benefit them long after the presenter has left the meeting.

The Learning Environment

If you have ever been in a learning audience with a poorly executed set-up for interaction, you know how it feels when the leader says, "OK, go find somebody and talk about what you just learned." Help! That's pretty broad and fairly threatening—especially to the introverts in the group—which is most of the population! A skilled facilitator is indeed gentle with the set-up, using phrases such as, "Let's try something" or "Bear with me while I explain a bit what I'd like you to do."

Author Geoff Bellman of many books on training and communication is a master at this. When you see him present at large training conferences, these phrases are part of his script. He gets huge crowds interacting willingly and immediately. He is gentle, clear, and uses his natural humor to cajole.

The fearless facilitator uses his or her comparative advantage over the group—perhaps humor, artistic ability, musical talent, or enthusiasm for reliable data—to create a fun, welcoming environment for participation.

Most of us have had difficult audiences in meetings or workshops or retreats. Cyndi once trained firefighters in communication skills for over three years for a suburban municipality. That was her "battleground" for trial and error in the skill of gentle activity and interaction set-up. With these firefighters, teamwork was natural, just not in the classroom! Cyndi learned to clarify the reasoning for every interactive discussion, gently and with humor, to make the point of the activity crystal-clear. Setting up the learning environment for this group was one of her most challenging tasks, but she learned it could be done, as can you. She was able to help them articulate what they were doing that made them such a good team. Like the "hot wash" technique used by some in the military, she helped them see what they were actually doing that appeared to be natural. In fact, it was an intricate choreography of skills that would aid them in getting better, in correcting errors, and in on-boarding new recruits.

Consider these ideas to help you set up the learning environment. Once you see them work for you, you may never look back!

Think Outcome for the Audience, Not Slide Deck

When you focus on the audience and what you want them to learn and value from your presentation, you are rightly focused. While your presentation will have some aspects of a performance, the most important thing that can happen from you being there is not the evaluations or adulation you receive. It is the outcome, the result, and the transformation that the audience experiences.

Trust Your Audience to Learn, Even If They Do Not Yet Know How or Why

Given the opportunity, all audiences want to learn. Not all of them will sit still as you talk on and on and on. There is no need to risk their distraction. Involve them as you would a friend in a conversation.

Touch Your Audience; Don't Just Talk to Them

Ghandi said the longest journey is from the head to the heart. Audiences, even tough ones, want to be touched, not just talked at. Use emotion, story, and interaction to help them understand and feel the importance of the message.

Kevin was presenting to an audience of doctors in the pharmaceutical industry—research-oriented, data-driven, hard-nosed experts—and during one brief facilitation exercise, a physician said, "You know why I'm working on this drug? Because I believe it would have saved my wife's life. I want to help someone else keep his wife alive." What he said connected the rest of the audience to the exercise more than any data or lecture could have. They were moved.

Treat them as treasured guests . . . not as adoring fans or resentful, required, and resistant registrants (even if they are!). The more gracious you are, the more involved they will be; the more encouraging you are, the harder it will be for them to resist your charms; and the more you give them a chance to learn and grow, the more you'll see them blossom. A famous speaker recently confided to an audience of his peers, "I used to speak to get affection because I did not know how to love another person, so I let my audiences fill that need." He went on to tell us what a mistake he had made. We knew him before and after this transformation, and he was right. His recognition of this lack in himself and his focus on the wrong thing changed him for the better.

Train Yourself to Think About the Others, Not About You

This is often the hardest part for traditional presenters, especially experts who think they "know" what the audience needs. Imagine you are a world-class expert. A subject-matter expert once told us, "I am the second greatest expert on this topic in the world. I will be number 1 as soon as my teacher dies!" He said this with a straight face and without compunction. Some of us are experts. There is no need, however, to think that the audience has nothing to say on the subject (no matter how needy or adoring). Experts—driven by ego, tradition, or ignorance—treat their audiences as if they are force-feeding them, not knowing that people rarely retain much of our material. However, they retain a great deal of the experience and of their interpretation of the experience.

Try Techniques That Will Start Them Talking to One Another; Don't Cave In to Distrusting Yourself and Distrusting Them

Be creative. Allow yourself to make a mistake, to mess up from time to time, or to not do it "just right" once in a while. What we have learned is that we notice, even when the audience does not. Kevin once tried a new technique for him, to answer questions briefly in "threes." Essentially, this technique suggests that for every question, we can respond by saying, "Well, there are three reasons why. . . ." This technique allows us to be succinct with our answers and our audiences to grasp the main elements. For example, if someone asked us, "Why is facilitating important?" we could go on and on about our theory and practice, giving them this entire book! What if we instead responded, "There are three reasons; first, success . . . your presentation will be more effective; second, outcomes . . . your audience will learn more; and third, applause . . . your evaluations will jump for the sky!"

Several years ago, Kevin was answering his first question in "threes" and told the first, then the second, and—halfway through the second part—he blanked on what the third part should be. What to do? He facilitated! Looking at the audience, he said, "Before I tell you my third thing, what do you think my third thing is?" Five hands went up in the air. Always trust your audience!

You Can Always Facilitate, No Matter the Circumstances

Rarely are there times when you would not want to have the audience facilitated . . . and after a great deal of thought, we can't think of any! Well, how about:

A fifteen-minute commencement speech? Popular commencement speakers facilitate well, for they do so with stealth! Peppering their talk with stories about the graduates, their parents, and famous watering holes allows the audience to dream, enjoy, and mirror the memory with the speaker. They are not in groups of two; they are grouped as a stadium together.

A ten-minute update for your team? Call the attendees in advance and ask what they most want to hear from your update. You will have their attention because they helped you and you are talking about what they want.

A eulogy for a family friend or relative? Attend the wake and interview everyone. Then incorporate these exact quotes in your eulogy. Open with your story, but spend most of your time on their memories and quotes. You will have them and hold them throughout.

The wedding toast? Be careful not to make this one big "in" joke with references only a few guests understand. Wedding toasts and eulogies are no different except that the target of your affection is alive! Always let your audience help you write your speech.

The launch of a new product to 150 eager sales professionals? Show your enthusiasm, but do not neglect moving them into small groups to react, respond, and renew their own enthusiasm. Speak from the frame of mind that your job is to "activate" (not to "motivate") them.

We still can't think of any time facilitation is not appropriate, but how about:

A one-on-one conversation with your spouse? You'd better make time to listen here!

Talking to your adolescent who comes in at 2 a.m.? Resist doing what he or she expects. Instead, make hot chocolate and talk about what he or she liked most about the evening. Your child will come around soon enough to what you might really want to talk about. Never be predictable . . . especially to an audience of that one adolescent who knows you better than anyone else, or thinks so at least!

Listening to your doctor give bad news? Interrupt and ask questions. Bring a relative with you who can keep his or her wits. Ask the doctor, "What questions would you have if you were me?" or "What was the best question asked by your last patient with this diagnosis?"

Preaching a sermon to a full congregation? Don't kid yourself. Preachers do this to us all the time, even though we are pinned to our pews. They use eye contact, emotion, humor, story, and some wandering down the aisle, touching kids, and gesturing broadly. They do this to make the message go down easier and to facilitate its incorporation into our actions for the week to come.

Being a TV or radio reporter? Pay attention to your favorite ones. How do they draw you into their report? What do they do with their eyes, the nodding of their heads, the look, the pause, their hands, and even their choice of words? Pay attention to how they draw you in, even though you can't talk to them.

The fact is that every interaction is an opportunity for interaction! It is in the interacting that we learn from, that we retain, and that we can actually do something with the material that has been shared through the interaction.

The fearless facilitator is someone who knows there is risk. Of course there is! When you open yourself to dialogue, there is always risk. And coming with the risk is new learning, feedback, partnership, and movement.

Lessons from One Executive's Transformation

One of our coaching clients wanted to transform not only her meetings but also her executive presence in meetings, in one-on-one interactions, even at home, where she had a very busy, active family. She is a smart person, and her success at work has come largely through her intellect and her hard work. She leaves nothing to chance and is a strong, dominant personality. She is admired but not liked; seen as competent, but not warm; and while her boss likes the work that's done, her peers sometimes feel left out or surpassed.

All of this did not make for someone who would learn and experiment with the skills of facilitation easily. How would you feel? Your success, even your reputation, has been built on being a one-woman show, and yet you know there is a nagging presence inside that says, despite your success, you are playing a zero sum game.

She did what we always recommend. She started small and slow and without a show. We asked her where she wanted to begin, and her choice was to begin with her executive presence at meetings. Not all facilitation means you are the presenter. She was concerned (and had received direct feedback from her boss) that at some meetings she was too quiet, at others too talkative, and at still others was seen as arrogant. She was quiet when superiors were around; over-talked with her peers; and was perceived as arrogant when she was with those who reported to her. Our analysis of each of these behaviors boiled down to the same issue—control. She was a first born in her family, had remarkable school success, and received almost all of her "goodies" by being superior at anything she chose to accomplish; she just wasn't always aware of how she was seen by others.

She wasn't happy, however, both by her own evaluation and certainly by her boss's recent comments. She knew (and we knew) that if she was to be perceived as a true leader, she was going to have to cope with the issue of control and its many manifestations.

She decided to do three things immediately at every meeting, whether with her superiors, her peers, or her staff:

First, she resolved to come into every meeting with a 3x5 card that had three things she wanted to contribute to every meeting. This helped her speak up with her superiors, become more succinct with her peers, and focus better with her staff. In essence, she was preparing for each meeting by doing the same activity. Fearless facilitators do the same thing when they are preparing to present. Their presentation is less about their slides and more about the three things they most want the audience to take from their slides.

Next, she decided to begin every response to someone else with a type of encouragement. These often took the form of:

- "You know what I liked about what you just said was. . . . "
- "I appreciate. . . ."
- "I learned _____ from you about _____ ."
- "Thank you for your emphasis on. . . ."

This encouragement gave her new access to every one of the three groups she knew she had to impact. Even when she disagreed, she was able to use a technique Susan Campbell writes about in her book, *Saying What's Real*.

- "I have a different idea. May I share it with you?" Or if you are 180 degrees different, say: "I have a slightly different idea!"

- "I appreciate your concern about _____ and I'd like to get some things out in the open. Would that be OK with you?"

- "Hearing you say that, I am reminded of. . . ."

Prior to this change, she was a person who minced few words. She went right to the heart of things and put many people off or discouraged any initiative they might ever have had.

So far, neither of the two things she tried took her out of her arena of control. In fact, the initial response of others was so positive she felt very successful. (Other members of her team wondered what happy pill she was taking!) Then we asked her to do something very difficult for her—to ask questions and listen rather than give answers and directions. This was hard for her and for her staff, and husband, and children, and her dog! We encouraged her, however, to attempt to succeed in an area she was not so good at. This was harder for her, but she was an achiever by heart, never passed up getting an "A" grade, so we were confident she could succeed. This took longer, but she perceived it as the exact skill her superiors used with her, which was her ticket. When she made the connection between what her bosses did and what she needed to do, something clicked and it clicked big time!

Last, she became a fearless listener!

The set-up is important because it is the equivalent of your dentist telling you how far to open your mouth, your doctor asking you to lie down a certain way for an examination, or your dancing teacher telling you where to place your hands with your partner. Clarity is important, but so is the long view every fearless facilitator must take: What is at stake here? Who are these people? What do they need? and How can I be useful to them?

Coach's Comments

- How do I set up a facilitation "gently"?

While you don't want to err on the side of being abrupt, you also don't want to be too careful either. The goal is to respect your audience in all that you do and say. Every time you ask them to move into groups, give only one instruction at a time:

"When I give you the signal, I'd like you to find one other person who is not at your table and go sit with that person."

"I'd like you to turn your chair toward your partner."

"I'll give you three minutes. Please discuss _____ with your partner."

Some facilitators give all three instructions at once, and this confuses most audiences. While you are telling them what to discuss, they are focused on whom they will sit with! Group psychology reigns in this situation. Smart people will not look so smart if you load them down with too much information all at once.

Take it one step at a time.

- What's the difference in preparing an agenda for facilitation compared with what I would prepare for a presentation?

This depends on the outcome you want, the audience, the content, and the venue. As a general rule, give some thought to what you think would be useful for the audience. What do they want to talk about? What do they need to talk about?

For example, let's say you have a room full of hospital executives who are preparing to build a new wing of the hospital. In a traditional model, they would be in a U-shape setting with an architect, engineer, project manager, and contractor each giving extensive PowerPoint or keynote presentations to an audience that occasionally may ask a question.

Now, imagine you only have executives there for the first meeting. You put them in groups of three or four and ask, "Remember the last time you remodeled anything in your home. What three things did you learn from that experience?" Give them time to talk, have them record their ideas on flip charts, one per group. Then conduct a discussion (and it is likely to be a lively one!) about what they learned and what they would do differently. Typical responses could be like these:

"It cost twice as much as we anticipated."

"The contractors' time schedule was off. Sometimes, the workmen didn't show up."

"Everyone had ideas after we started so the plans needed to be changed and that cost money."

"It wasn't until we were done that we learned better ideas!"

"I tried doing some of it myself and well. . . ."

"I'm never going to do that again!"

Now, you have the beginnings of a discussion involving the people who will actually be responsible for the building. Can you imagine the questions the architect, engineer, project manager, and contractor will have to answer at meeting number two?

One executive finished this exercise by saying, "Well, now our family is building something special. Let's plan to do it right, on time, and on budget. Let's build something we will all be proud of."

This group is ready not because they know all the specifications yet. They are ready because their heads and hearts are in it.

- How should I arrange the room?

Facilitation can take place in any space. Few, if any, tables are best since you can move chairs around the room for small group discussions, work sessions, etc. U-shape, half-rounds, classroom style with long tables, even auditoriums will work, but they will be more uncomfortable and distracting.

Many planners and hotel professionals will automatically plan for round tables or a U-shape set-up unless you tell them you only want chairs. We've fought many a battle for "chairs only" and then, after the event, the planner tells us what a great idea it was to eliminate the tables! Remember that it is your meeting!

- What is a value interpreter?

Your audience decides what was useful, period. While we may have stellar information and media, expertise, and handouts, even cutting-edge research, it is the audience who decides and interprets what was good for them. The value interpretation rests with them alone. Some presenters blame the audience for being slow, lame, or uninvolved. In truth, the hard truth, it is the presenter's job to adapt to the audience. It is not the audience's job to conform to the presenter.

Many times, the audience sees real value when they encounter a chance to actively learn as well as listen. After a full day of facilitation with very little lecturing, one of Kevin's participants said, "Wow, that was a great lecture!" What he meant was that it was a meaningful experience for him. Kevin just said, "Thank you!"

- How do I explain to my reluctant team that this new format is worth trying?

How about not explaining and just doing it? When it is your time to present, facilitate a bit. You can even do this when you have your internal meetings with your team. Don't tell them you are going to facilitate and then . . . facilitate. Some will catch on, others may not see it, but our experience is that it is a highly positive experience.

You may have some naysayers who will find reasons not to do it even in the face of success. The excuses will sound very tempting: the CEO will be there, the audience is full of Ph.D.s, the doctors are all surgeons, what if they all walk out, etc. One tactic you can use is to ask for their trust. "Let me try this. If it doesn't work for this meeting, then we can discuss it." Note we didn't say, "I'll never do it again." We just left it open for discussion.

All of the following resources provide convincing arguments to counter the skeptics. Make sure you read them first:

- www.theworldcafe.com

- www.openspaceworld.org

- The book, *Open Space Technology: A User's Guide* by Harrison Owen.

- What if someone is thinking something that would enhance the conversation but won't share it? Even when I ask directly, the person still won't talk?

Respect is the key here. There are many reasons that someone will not share. We have to respect that choice. Most audience members will share once they feel comfortable.

Other options might include: groups of three for one question, a new group of three for the second one, and a new group for the third. This allows every person to meet and speak with six others. Often those who are reticent to speak in a large group will do so in a smaller group, will listen to their peers, and will feel more comfortable. And then they'll end up sharing!

Attorneys know that the last 10 percent of any conversation is the most important. Clients and potential clients usually reveal the most in those final moments. This is when attorneys will listen most closely. Counselors and family therapists know this also. Often, after thirty, forty, even fifty minutes of a meeting, their clients will reveal something very important.

The same could be true with your reluctant audience members. They may be waiting and waiting for a very good reason unknown to us. Our job is to be respectfully patient. Our job is also to focus on those who do want to share, and when we do our job well, there will be plenty of them.

Seven

Listen Live, Then Disappear!

"To get people to think without lecturing to them, I prepare a set of questions beforehand. This generates some energy in the room and people begin to think about the subject, not just listen. This energy I'm trying to create is not only between me and the group I'm addressing, but more importantly, between the group members themselves. When this interaction between group members is really happening, I turn from lecturer to guide, and then lead the group through the discussion topic. A by-product of this type of dynamic group process is the generation of an idea or ideas that I've never considered. When it's all over, the group leaves feeling like participants, and are more likely to remember the topic and the discussion that took place."

—*Ricky C. Tanksley, Chief of Police, Oak Park Police Department, Oak Park, Illinois*

- Learn from the skilled listening of veteran talk-show hosts, journalists, sales professionals, and orchestra conductors.

- Be ready to respond ably to unexpected or difficult comments or questions.

- Be patient and trust that audience wisdom will be revealed.

What Oprah and Larry Know

The best facilitators, even those with super-star power, "disappear." What Oprah Winfrey, Larry King, the crew from "60 Minutes"—even your local Montessori teacher—know is how to disappear behind questions. In their interviews, their questions are usually brilliant, but it's what they're doing during the answers that is even more admirable. They are truly listening "in the moment," ready for any answer they may receive. It is because of this "live listening" that they retrieve their best and most engaging interviews.

Similarly, when facilitators are "listening live"—with energy, concentration, and intense awareness—they retrieve their best and most engaging involvement. Most people like hearing what they and others in the group have to say as much as if not more than what the facilitator has prepared. The best facilitators know this to be true and therefore focus most of their energy and thought process on "live listening."

Here are some steps to achieve more involvement:

- *Be among the group.* Any time you have an opportunity to leave the front or the stage area of your room, do so. During discussion or group work, use "purposeful wandering." To the untrained eye, you are simply walking among the audience, but to the trained facilitator you are "listening live."

- *Nod to acknowledge silently.* Watch any good facilitator as he or she wanders the room and you will notice that he or she wears a pleasant expression and is nodding frequently as he or she listens. Over-nodding looks false, but frequent, sincere nodding lets the participants know you're with them.

- *Comment frequently on their responses.* If people are working in groups, brief comments such as, "Good thinking" or "You are on track" can easily insert encouragement. You can guide as well with comments like, "May I suggest you think more specifically about your own area?" or "Good, and try to apply that last concept we discussed as well."

- *Compliment more often than you may be used to.* The best compliments are specific, task-related, and of course, genuine, such as, "Sarah, I especially like the way you're probing for more information" or "Wayne and Sam, you are doing especially well relating to the mission." When you are this specific, you are really encouraging the person to do more. To tell someone he is doing a good job is certainly nice. To tell someone specifically what you notice about her skills related to the job; that is encouraging and will likely help her use these skills even more in the future.

- *Say "Thank you."* Saying "thank you" is one of the most neutral ways to acknowledge contributions and is even better than, "Good point." If you say "Good point" too often, it loses its meaning. It also becomes the standard, so even irrelevant contributions are labeled as "good." Far better for you to remain neutral with a sincere "thank you," which allows the group to decide what is "good" or not.

- *Acknowledge first contributors.* Some presenters will provide small prizes or a free book to first contributors, but fearless facilitators often use a simple "Thank you for going first." It is not easy to speak first, and the rest of the group knows this, too. The value of you acknowledging it allows the group to see the value and allows the person to be recognized as a "fearless participant"!

When you can be aware enough of what is happening in your group to call out the contributors, to notice the most helpful metaphors, and to acknowledge the most on-target thought leaders in the group, others will begin to contribute their best ideas rather than throw everything that crosses their minds at the board. The result is a discussion focused on future results and a productive use of time.

Kevin had a group of specialized teachers who were working on approaches to bring their disparate schools together for more visibility and legislative influence. As the two-day meeting progressed, several people noted that they found they were getting to know each other better with fewer walls dividing them. It didn't take much to make the analogy that this experience of the group may inform how they will treat their legislators: by mail or personal contact! An easy choice once the experience informed their awareness.

What the Best Do Not Do

Professor Helen Meldrum from Bentley University in Massachusetts teaches the difference between listening and the "deadly four responses" that in our culture are frequently confused with true listening: judging, advising, quizzing, and placating.

Judging: "Do you really think that is a good idea?" When you judge, you aren't really listening to the other person, you are listening to what you would do, what your judgment is, what you think is best.

Advising: "If I were you. . . ." Here you are offering your wisdom and your counsel without being asked. The advice columnist, Ann Landers, once said that she never gave advice to anyone unless he or she asked or unless she dressed twins alike! (Ann was a twin, with issues!)

Quizzing: "Don't you think you ought to. . . ." This quizzing technique is a great blend of judging and advising in the form of a potentially harmless question. Actually, it is a leading question. Consider, would you rather be the one in the witness box answering the question or the one asking it?

Placating: "I can see how you might have thought that was a good idea." Here you are patting the person on the head as some do to a child and taking a superior stance, in effect, saying, "You poor misguided thing. I can help you be better!"

These deadly four mask themselves as listening responses when in fact they do two things that are just the opposite: they allow us to talk instead of listen and, worse, they convey to others our importance instead of theirs. This is vitally important for the fearless facilitator to understand. We really have to trust the wisdom of the group and convey with our every move that we believe in them to the core. We do this best when we operate on a horizontal plane of communication, that we are all social equals, worthy of our stories being heard, we can all contribute to the whole. When we operate on a vertical plane where one is higher or lower than the others, then we tend to value those above, talk down to those below, and compete for attention, recognition, and the microphone!

The true fearless facilitator who listens works to achieve a most special kind of mastery here. It is not so much a technique as it is a tuning in to your audience. Yes, you will use the skills of listening. You will also use the "mojo" of listening—that most special fluency of purpose, attentiveness, and responsiveness that invites the audience to a new kind of learning, a community of learning that endures well past our ending.

The fearless facilitator learns to "tune in" to the audience on a horizontal plane.

What the Journalist Uncovers

The facilitator can learn about "listening live" from the journalist. Great journalists are trained to "disappear" behind the question. By creating a non-threatening interview, they uncover information that may lie beneath the surface.

Imagine how the reporter for the Bloomington, Indiana, newspaper *The Herald Times*, felt when she retrieved this gem from a seasoned female police officer about another female officer who had died that week at age seventy-nine: "We wore plain clothes as detectives," she said, reminiscing about the 1950s. "Barb had on high heels with the ankle strap around them—those were fashionable then. And Barb, who was not afraid of the devil himself, jumped in that car and pulled the young lady out, and when Barb got out, the shoes were off her feet but they were still buckled around her ankle and were hanging off her ankles. It's kind of hard to maintain a real stern, 'I'm an officer of the law,' with your shoes hanging off your ankles."

So what could have been a rather boring tribute to a veteran cop became a telling tribute to the challenges women police officers faced in those days. Anyone who facilitates sessions with female police officers would be delighted to uncover a story like this. And this is what the journalist knows.

The fearless facilitator uncovers the nearly forgotten stories and lessons learned.

What the Orchestra Conductor Knows

The facilitator is a guide; many professional facilitators may or may not be subject-matter experts, but what they all have in common is that they are listening experts, hired for bringing forth the wisdom of others—to form a learning community. As the conductor of an orchestra knows, the most stellar performances come from the ability to elicit the best sounds from each instrument—with the right cadence, tone, emotion, and timing. Similarly, the facilitator controls the cadence, tone, emotion, and timing of the discussion. In an orchestra, the musicians are the performers, not the conductor.

In a well-facilitated discussion, the audience shares its best knowledge, not the facilitator. A trainer imparts knowledge; a keynote speaker performs, entertains, and motivates, but a facilitator simply guides and engages.

Here is how they do it (and what they also avoid doing) in order to bring the best out of others. Dr. Domeena Renshaw, MD, from Loyola University Stritch School of Medicine boils it all down to four key ingredients:

1. Trust

This is the basis of all human relationships. While other relationships have time to gain this trust, fearless facilitators have precious little time to gain it. Therefore, they do two things early and often—demonstrate interest one-to-one and create a sense of group identity. Many facilitators achieve the first by shaking as many hands as possible, meeting as many in the group as soon as they can, and making eye contact with as many one-to-one as possible. When you do this, you create an ally who will root for you. President Lyndon Johnson once remarked that every handshake is worth 250 votes. Although he was very powerful, he was also very convincing to others when he wanted to get something done one-to-one.

Facilitators also create a sense of community by knowing why the group has come together, and they use that information early and often. For example, although a group of professionals may be gathering at their annual meeting for educational programs, what they are "really" there for may be landing a sale, seeing an old friend, or simply experiencing a good time with those who understand the business. This is why some speakers at these meetings regard themselves as "edutainers," feeling that, although they may be there to educate, they are really there to entertain. Our view is different: facilitators are there to form and profile the learning community and in that process they educate, entertain, and create an enduring memory of the attendees themselves.

What they do not do is think that their enthusiasm, their humor, or their signature stories will alone bring the group together. The ego of fearless facilitators is quite hidden, as they are there to form a "we" not a "me."

2. Touch

Dr. Renshaw is a psychiatrist and was a forerunner in the field of sexual dysfunction, quite famous and very approachable. While she advocated physical touch for her patients, she also had the rare ability to walk into a room, to greet a colleague, to speak with and to a group, and to give the impression that she "touched" each and every person. In fact, many years later, colleagues who were her former students, physicians, nurses, and psychologists would all, on the mention of her name, have a soft smile and speak about how she "touched" them in their time of formation and need.

Facilitators need to be very aware of how they touch others in a non-physical way. Moving around the room and being close by is a form of touching. Bringing the hand-held microphone to a contributor is a form of touching. Paraphrasing accurately touches in a most special way: questioners hear themselves again! While performers and those giving traditional speeches may touch us with their songs, dances, or messages, it is only skilled facilitators who can guarantee the touch by how they "are" with the participants.

What the facilitator does not do is to take this for granted, to invade the audience, to volunteer others, to call out names to ask questions on the spot, or to jokingly make fun of someone's error or uniqueness. Facilitators are "respecters" to the max. They jealously guard their respect for every person in the audience, they thrive on it, and they do this above all else. Audiences will forgive you for anything except disrespect.

3. Time

Fearless facilitators are keenly aware of time without even mentioning it. Like a gambling casino without clocks, the facilitator is quietly aware of what has to be done when, without any outward concern. If time runs short, fearless facilitators cut their goals down to size. If someone is going on and on and on, they adjust. If the group takes a useful departure from the plan, they go with them. Of course, this is not easy to do. It is much easier if we can plot out exactly what will happen when, and—to a certain extent—we can do this. The fearless facilitator, however, is flexibility incarnate! Like being served a meal in first class on the plane or at a fine restaurant, we are taking all the time we want. The flight attendant, chef, and waiter all know precisely about time and use it, however silently, to their advantage.

What fearless facilitators do not do is call attention to time. You wouldn't hear them say, "We have to stop pretty soon. We are running short of time." Or "the only thing between you and lunch is me" or any of the hundreds of useless time references we and you have heard over the years. If time is running short, then shorten up the program; don't try to stuff ten pounds in a five-pound sack.

Fearless facilitators can work their magic in five days, one day, six hours, or fifteen minutes. What they do is plan accordingly. What they do not do is try to be and do everything. It is certainly OK to leave the audience wanting more; in fact, it is preferred!

4. Talk

By now, you likely know what we think of talking! We are in favor of it . . . just not too much of it! Well-directed, well-punctuated, well-focused, and well-used talk is one of the fearless facilitator's best allies. The talk only has to mean something and has to be completely directed toward the ultimate goal. This is the most difficult skill fearless (and fearful!) facilitators, new and experienced, are faced with every day:

- "How much should I say here?"

- "Is it time for me to redirect the conversation?"

- "Was that last contributor's remark something I need to say something about?"

- "What do they need to hear from me, and when, and how?"
  (Perhaps the ultimate talk question for the fearless facilitator!)

Ambrose Bierce defined a bore as a person who talks when you wish him to listen. It is a delicate thing!

The fearless facilitator, like the orchestra conductor, knows how to get the best sounds from each "instrument" or person in the room through techniques that build trust.

What the Sales Professional Knows

Dianna Booher, a veteran speaker and prolific author, admits that she hates to sell, but loves to help people. Early in her career, a manager taught her to frame a mindset of helping rather than selling, which buoyed her to overcome her dread of sales. She learned to listen well to potential clients, ask them questions to determine all the nuances of their problem, and—most important—tell them from the outset that she would let them know whether she was the right fit for their needs. With this mindset, the sale became less a sale and more a facilitated needs analysis.

Similarly, the best facilitators ask questions to get at the heart of any need, issue, or problem that is under the surface of the meeting. Professional coaches and counselors are well schooled in this area, and facilitators can learn from their techniques. Counselors learn to listen for repeated themes as well as the nonverbal communication that accompanies those themes. Counselors speak most frequently to steer and suggest, rather than to judge or prescribe.

Questions can also help to keep us from being judgmental, from attempting to be "right," and allow us to be curious, affirming, and educational all at the same time. Eugene Ionesco said it best: "It is not the answer that enlightens, but the question." Good sales professionals engage in similar techniques as they decipher the true needs of the potential customer.

The fearless facilitator makes the discussion easy by asking good questions.

Really Good Facilitators Use These Questions

Open-Ended Questions

These are questions that cannot be answered with a simple "yes" or a "no." They can be based on facts or feelings using the familiar what, why, when, where, who, and how. "Can you tell us more about that?" and "Would you give us an example" are common, effective, open-ended questions that elicit more from the participant for the benefit of the larger group.

Closed-Ended Questions

These questions can be answered with a simple "yes" or "no." The purpose of these questions is two-fold: first, to confirm information and second, to regain the conversation ball and put things right back in your lap! You can use this kind of a question to change the conversation, to quiet the conversation, or simply to have the ability to move to the next item on the agenda or plan. These kinds of questions are often used by the police, by attorneys, and by angry parents! They are not routinely used to establish rapport, empathy, or a lengthy response!

Reflective Questions

These questions are similar to a paraphrase but with a question attached. They show that you listened, help keep the focus on the other person, can engage the other beyond rapport, create connection, and often cement the relationship: "So it sounds like, given all that you have said about your experience camping, that it has become a family interest as well?" This then leads to a closed-ended question with the rapport of an open-ended one! "I like what you said about your experience with your visit to Congress, and it makes me think that you might want to do this again in the future. Can you tell us whether that is correct and what seemed to engage you so much?" This is a reflective leading to an open-ended question.

Affirmative Questions

The purpose of these questions is to affirm the other, which sends a safe message to a perhaps hesitant participant or group of participants. "I love your description of that meeting. It helps me understand what you were walking into. Can you tell us what happened next?" While the affirmative question can help the shy, cautious, or conservative participant, it is also just as useful on the engaged, more open participant. One client said of her boss, "Yes, he really does like to be affirmed!" Don't we all!

The caution here is to avoid falling into the traditional facilitator and presenter clichés: "Great question." "Great answer." "Wow, wasn't that a terrific response?" Never praise your participants ("You are the best . . . so good . . . really smart . . . best ever," etc.).

Instead, encourage them by beginning with "I appreciate," "I learned," "I like," etc.

> The fearless facilitator understands that praise feels good for a fleeting moment, but encouragement leaves a lasting impact.

In a marathon, praise is what you reserve for the one and only winner of the race; encouragement is what you say to the runners as they pass by who are achieving their goals.

Fact-Finding Questions

These informative, simple queries are easy to answer, designed to relax the other, and build rapport and comfort (as long as you don't sound like you are compiling a list or a prosecuting attorney!). Rapport and interest are vital elements here. The other person has to feel your connection, or you will come across as "creepy."

While waiting outside a mosque on his first day in Istanbul, Kevin was befriended by an engaging, friendly local who asked where he was from, followed by details and praise about Chicago. After a few minutes of this friendly fact-filled chat, he said to Kevin, "You like rugs? I have a shop not far from here. Very cheap!" Kevin then understood the reason for the conversation. When Kevin replied "No, thank you," the man smiled and wily said, "I think you are lying. Everyone from Chicago loves rugs!" Maybe not creepy, but certainly it was time for Kevin to run!

Fearless facilitators know that fact-finding questions are vital when learning about the audience, but they quickly transition to questions that will more deeply engage and connect.

Educational Questions

Schools are now coupling these questions with audience-response technology that displays what percentage of the audience had each correct. These are a great way to measure how well the audience comprehends the content. The technology embarrasses no one, because the voting is anonymous.

Depending on the outcome, we call these teachers "fearless professors" because the students' accuracy directly relates to the effectiveness of the lecture just given!

Feeling-Finding Questions

These solicit strongly held and personal issues, such as attitudes, opinions, motivations, hidden agendas, family disputes, timelines, politics, and prejudices. When someone is going on and on about how "he did this to me" and "what I did to her," you can help redirect the flow and amount of detail by saying, "And how did that make you feel?" or, if humor is needed, you can say, "Sounds like you have some feelings about that."

While there are hundreds of feeling words, they typically fall into one of five categories, which can help us readily sum up our understanding of the participants. These words are *sad, mad, glad, scared,* and *hurt.* When someone is telling us a fact-filled story about losing an aging dog to cancer, we can show both empathy and understanding with: "You were really sad when you had to put her down." Just be prepared for the other person to respond: "No! I was furious with the vet who missed the initial diagnosis!" Then you reply, "You were mad. This death didn't have to happen as it did."

Whether using one-to-one conversations or facilitating a whole room, the job of the feeling response is to show understanding and to connect on the level that helps the other person feel more completely understood. As Alfred Adler wrote, feelings are the gas in our tank, and while we don't want them in the driver's seat, they do provide the fuel for our decisions and actions. Going back to that restaurant where they didn't treat you so well?

Buying that same kind of car that turned out to be a lemon? Ever go grocery shopping on an empty stomach? You get the picture!

Really Good Facilitators Avoid These Questions
Complicated Questions

"Let me ask you how you got to the meeting, and what happened there. I wonder how you felt when she attacked you, and what the ramifications are of that meeting, and finally, what you did and felt. And was Bob there?"

Believe it or not, this is a very common interviewer error. You can even hear it on radio and television. The interviewer is so unfocused that he or she un-focuses the respondent!

If you are ever asked this kind of a question, follow former Defense Secretary Robert McNamara's advice: "Don't answer the question they asked you; answer the question you wished they had asked you!" There is tremendous skill and skilled discipline in asking simple, direct, and uncomplicated questions.

Repetitious Questions

"So I was wondering how you got there. I mean, did you fly or drive or, you know, did you get there in a particular way given how much traffic and how flying is these days. And, you know, it just seemed to me this would have been tough to do, getting there I mean." Yes, this could go on forever!

Ask a simple question and then shut up!

Fearless facilitators understand that the most candid, introspective answers come from the simplest of questions.

Leading Questions

Lawyers try to get away with this one: "Isn't it true you never wanted to do this project in the first place?" If you want a defensive answer and a disconnected colleague, this is a sure-fire way to get it.

Suggestive Questions

No, we don't mean that kind! Suggestive here refers to suggesting the answer to the other person . . . again, a highly misused way of asking. "So when you went to India, were you there for business, pleasure, curiosity, as a hobby; I mean, were you there for fun or did you go for lack of anything better to do, maybe visit friends?"

Or simply (please!) say: "What brought you to India?" (Then listen!)

Ego Questions

"Let me ask you about your children. When I had kids I was very clear with them about who was boss. I made sure each of them did what I wanted. Spare the rod; spoil the child, if you know what I mean. So, with your children, I wondered if you were able to get that kind of grip on them?"

Yes, all of his kids went to college at eighteen and never came home again! (And he didn't obtain a good answer to whatever his question was!)

In All of Your Meetings

Plan and Prepare

While you cannot plan what they will say or do, you can lay out a plan for what you will say, what you will do, and when you will engage them. It is important that you have some outline in your head that adds structure to the freedom facilitation gives to the attendees. This structure cannot be so tight that it constricts and not so loose that it is undetectable.

Outcomes

You'll need to know what you want to accomplish (as well as what they want), as well as the timelines that need to be respected. Whatever you do, whatever the outcomes, never go overtime! Never, ever, never! This is one faux pas for which you will never, ever be forgiven. (Worse than going overtime is telling them that you are going overtime!)

Story

This is more nebulous but very important. The data, the PowerPoint slides, the flip charts, and the discussion have to be monitored by you as an ongoing story. You will be in charge of a simple, key message that links everything together. It can be as simple as, "We are leaders and our work is to get this done" or as seemingly complex as, "We need to figure this out." You may know the story line ahead of time or you may not. It may emerge from a participant or from an exercise or you thinking about it over lunch. You, however, must attend to it, for no one else will.

Invite and Involve

Your personal attention to each member of the audience, no matter how large or small, is absolutely critical to your success and to theirs. Watch good facilitators and you will know that they are observing beyond the others, listening deeper, and probing with simple, important questions. Kevin had the attention of a small group of twenty for one hour. He had never met any of them, but he had a hunch and said, "Mike, are you and Kathy married to each other?" The crowd roared. Mike said, "You don't know what you just said!" It turns out that it is the favorite joke of the team that, since their reorganization, the two communicated and conflicted like what they called "work spouses," and even their own real spouses laughed about it with them frequently. Beyond the joke and the laugh, they also talked about how they had to work harder to make sure that they really did work cooperatively and didn't assume too much from one another. (They sure did talk to each other like they were married!) This allowed the group to invite Kevin in on their inside joke, creating a more intimate, involved experience.

Ask and Listen

By now you know that we think this is skill number 1 for the fearless facilitator. Here we give it a special meaning, because the facilitator is the model of what should be, how it should be done, and what can be accomplished when done well. Asking can also be done non-verbally as well. Kevin recently led a program

(Continued)

(Continued)

in which the new CEO attended with twenty-three of his staff. Everyone had a name tag, but the CEO put his in his pocket and said, "I don't do name tags." Kevin reminded himself to listen, non-verbally. Throughout a dynamic discussion of his staff, the CEO remained glued to his iPad, avoided any group interaction, occasionally scanned the group, and left as soon as he could. After the program, some staff told Kevin that this man had only recently taken over, announcing on day one that he was here to save the place financially. The staff, he said, should not expect any "touchy-feely stuff" from him. It was interesting how little they seemed to care about his non-involvement and how invisible he was. Although he was the CEO, he saw himself as a behind-the-scenes CFO, albeit one with no inkling of leadership. The staff did listen to him, as did Kevin. This was simply one more occasion when he missed an opportunity to lead. He'll save the place no doubt, but then what?

Affirm and Encourage

Adler said encouragement is one thing you can never overdo. Openly appreciate your extroverts' participation, privately affirm your quieter ones' deliberateness, enjoy your socializing crowd's light spirit, know how difficult open participation is for some, how easy for others, and appreciate how others take notes, organize, help you out. Remember, you facilitate from the moment you arrive until the moment you leave, so be an appreciating, encouraging presence.

Summarize and Add

Never add and then summarize. Keep your thoughts and conclusions to yourself until everyone else has weighed in. Doing so will make it mean more, you will have more context to speak to from their comments, a bigger picture to refer to, and you will have their attention. On a team of twenty pharmacists and someone with a doctorate in economics, the pharmacists formed a tight group, smart, engaged, and "pharmaceutical." They wondered a bit about the Ph.D. not being a PharmD! It turned out that he was the most influential member of the team. Every twenty minutes he would pull what Kevin called a "Columbo moment." Like the seemingly hapless television detective, he would say, "Let me see if I understand. . . ." He would then go on to summarize the previous twenty minutes. As he did, the PharmDs nodded in agreement, took notes, and paid attention. He only summarized! It wasn't until the end of the meeting that he offered his additional ideas for their consideration. Within a meeting or two, a PharmD would say, "Remember that idea that we had at the last meeting?" The man with the doctorate just gave a slight, knowing, and satisfied smile.

Follow Up

At breaks, at lunch, after the event, make sure you as the facilitator are following up with loose ends, next steps, and more affirmations. It may be up to you to help craft the next meeting, so that this meeting is a step along the way, not a one-time thing.

What Listening Live Is Not

We observed the opening keynoter at a women's conference who was obviously trying to involve and encourage the audience of young career women with lots of questions from the podium. Her theme was finding your self-worth, and she asked rapid-fire questions like, " What are your talents?" "How many of you have a great day at work every day?" "How many of you think you're great?" While the questions fit the theme, and at first the young women responded with lots of hands raised, the energy in the room slowly diminished as everyone realized that she wasn't really "hearing" the answers. She simply kept going with the fast pace of her over-memorized opening and the effect was "in your face," rather than one of listening.

Live listening must be sincere; it is active and empathic. It is never manipulative, over-rehearsed, or "canned." While good facilitators have many phrases and even short scripts that they use to encourage conversation and discussion, they never assume the response they may receive. The live listener asks the question with a sincere desire to understand the other's point of view—not to simply project to the next point, as the keynote speaker did. Her intent was to involve, but the result was distrust.

Fearless facilitators ask questions, not looking for a smooth transition to the next topic. Rather, fearless facilitators ask with a sincere desire to understand.

Timing Is Everything

Good discussion and decision making take time. Taking time not only engages and motivates, but it may also result in more ethical decisions. Recent studies at Northwestern University, Johns Hopkins University, and City University of Hong Kong revealed that, if employees are rushed when asked to make a choice between right and wrong, they are about five times more likely to make the unethical choice. "Given a fictitious situation in which they were asked to make an ethical decision and were offered more money for lying, most lied if given less than thirty seconds to decide," *Wall Street Journal* columnist Rachel Emma Silverman reported. "Those who had more time to think were much more likely to be truthful." This certainly serves as an alert to the facilitator: most people need time to think things through before making the best decision.

The "World Café" Discussion Technique

The "World Café" (www.theworldcafe.com) is a very effective facilitative exercise to elicit a wealth of real opinions when you have at least an hour to spend. We begin with the audience in groups of three discussing a topic related to the training or event. They work anywhere from three to fifteen minutes, and then we ask two group members to leave the group and join two other groups. Once new groups are formed, the arriving members share with the second group what they learned from the first group. We add a new discussion topic and repeat this process until everyone in the original group has moved on at least twice, always sharing with their new group what they learned from the previous group. The activity concludes with a charting and reporting of key ideas. This "world café" type of discussion has many benefits:

- Opinions are shared through reporting, which is more comfortable for less assertive people.

- Careful listening is required because members know they will be asked to report the key points to someone else.

- The real thoughts and feelings of the entire group are brought forth and compared.

- Diverse group members mingle in a safe, structured activity.

A side benefit, and often the highest benefit, of this technique is that every person in the room meets at least six others in a short space of time. Use this same technique for an entire day or multi-day experience and everyone will meet everyone! Remember, the role of the facilitator is to create a learning community. This technique nails that goal easily.

In this fast-paced world, it becomes more and more difficult to find appropriate discussion time for problem solving and opinion gathering. We respond to online surveys and chats; we are continually invited to review services and products; we are conditioned to provide our opinions quickly. But do we really listen to the thoughts of others first, without "script writing" what we'll say next?

The fearless facilitator avoids "script writing" what he or she will say next while listening.

The "Panel of Experts" Technique

This technique developed out of desperation. We were presenting a workshop to a group of mechanical contractors who were reluctant to participate in any of the planned discussions and activities. It wasn't that they were mean-spirited; they were just unaccustomed to on-the-job education with their bosses and co-workers. So we improvised by asking for the person who had been with the firm for the longest time, the shortest time, and at a midpoint in time to come forward. We quickly set up three chairs and called them our "Panel of Experts."

Then we simply asked the rest of the group what questions they would like to ask the "experts." We began with a few questions that fit the topic, such as "How would you advise a new hire?" and " What is the most important key to getting along in this company?" The activity worked very well because it was nonthreatening. There were no wrong answers. Since then, we use the "Panel of Experts" frequently because it's fun and no-fail.

The "Larry King" Interview Technique

This activity works well when you would like the group to get to know a leader or guest in a new way other than coffee-hour mingling. You need fifteen or twenty minutes, and we usually do this at the opening of the program. Be sure to ask the interviewee's permission in advance; let him or her know you'll be asking a series of nonthreatening questions to help the group get to know him or her. Warn your honored guest that these questions will include everything from family background to schooling to any company goals. Set up two chairs in front, and ask the interviewee to come forward. Before you begin, announce, "This a Larry King–type interview. Our guest today is _____. I have some questions in mind, but at times I'll ask for 'callers' as Larry used to do, and I hope you will respond with any questions you may have."

This activity is a no-fail choice because the facilitator controls it. Have a variety of questions from the light-hearted ("What were you like in high school?") to the serious ("What challenges do you see us facing in the months ahead?") Have plenty of questions just in case you receive one-word answers, as Larry himself often does! The audience "call-in" questions will give both you and the interviewee a good idea of what people really want to know. Often, the audience's questions will provoke more thought and insight than those you planned. Close the interview with them wanting more rather than letting it drag on too long.

The "Larry King Interview" is just one example of how you, as facilitator, can use the "natural resources" available to you—the people in the group.

The "secret sauce" to this technique comes at the end of the interview. Rather than offer your thanks, instead try this: "Now Mary is going to stop talking. If she does want to talk she can only say, 'Thank you,' and the rest of us are going to talk. We will all offer to her what we liked, learned, or appreciated about what she had to say in this brief time with her." Then watch the magic happen. This is especially affirming for the guest. Wait until all are finished, then add your own affirmation to close things out. Believe us on this one: it is a no-fail, all-gain activity, especially useful with the CEO, a person of power your team does not know well, or the executive who does not know your team well.

Your Natural Resources

Cyndi's brother, Therry, is a lifelong naturalist and expert on flora, fauna, and wildlife. To walk in the woods with him is an educational experience. He explains how everything in nature thrives in the right environment with simple natural resources. He shows how a rotting log lies in state to provide mulch and food for other creatures, how mayflowers need shade as much as buttercups need sun, and how birds make nests from the natural resources around them.

The naturalist's lessons apply for you as a facilitator as well. Your natural resources are the people with you in the room, and they thrive in the non-threatening environment you create. You do not need to import expensive "fertilizer"—games, incentives, speakers, and tools. True success will come from what is within, and that is what you will uncover when you "listen live."

Fearless facilitators seek out and appreciatively use the natural resources available to them: the people in the room.

Coach's Comments

- How can I become better at thinking on my feet during difficult situations?

If you don't have a lot of opportunity to field actual difficult questions, try setting up some practice role plays with a colleague. Think of a question that you ask your audience in a typical presentation, for example, "What is your number one sales challenge?" or "How is stress affecting your life?" Ask your partner to answer with something inappropriate such as, "I have no sales challenges" or "For stress, I drink a lot of alcohol." Then practice responding with the techniques described

(Continued)

in this chapter: neutral questions, outrageous comments, and "tag and add." Come up with as many practice questions as you can to be prepared for your next presentation. This is precisely the practice technique used by candidates for President of the United States (or should be!). Learning how to respond out loud (not in your head) is a humbling and useful exercise for all of us! Saying it is very different from thinking it indeed!

Another favorite of ours is to put yourself in fantasy positions and simply respond to the question of someone asking you to say a few words, to ask a probing question, to facilitate a group about a certain topic. At a wake, what if someone asked you to conduct the prayer service? At a wedding, what if you were asked to give the impromptu toast and somehow include everyone? If your boss were sick, what if you had to give the main points of his or her presentation? It's great mental practice, but remember that practicing out loud is the killer test of your mettle.

Eight

Go with It!

"In bringing together two departments that historically haven't played nice, my fears as a facilitator were daunting. What if they didn't like the exercises? Each other? Me? After spending time preparing, testing the format, and rehearsing, my nerves turned into energy. The participants responded well to the opportunity for open communication, and the follow-up surveys provided invaluable feedback that will help guide our next retreat."

—*Madalyn Kenney, Fundraising Professional*

- As the improvisation artist learns, go with the flow. One skill that will serve you well as you facilitate groups is to look a bit beyond and perhaps around the corner.

- Practice how not to over-think your answers Being a bit vague will help your audiences think better.

- Experience the power of your listening skills you will be able to improve with constant practice.

Take What They Give You

Improvisation actors and comedians say that one of the first skills they learn in comedy school is to say "yes . . . and" inside themselves, regardless of what line or situation is thrown at them. By doing so they keep themselves closely listening to their acting partners and responsive to what comes their way. The worst thing you can do to a skit or a fellow "improv" actor is to stop the action, question the cue, or become too logical. Your job is to go with what is given to you.

Trust!

Dr. Alan Kaplan, chief medical officer at Iowa Health Systems, wanted to be a better speaker and presenter. His job demanded that he present well, and his feedback was that he was falling short. Rather than enroll in a traditional speaking course, Alan enrolled in an improv class at a local comedy club and attended every week for a year! "It took me six months to loosen up," he said. "But now I can present and present well at the drop of a hat!"

The same is true for you. Trust yourself when you facilitate. Learn to "read" your audience. Trust your instincts. Know that you "know" them.

Fearless facilitators know their audiences before walking into the room, because they have pre-interviewed and spoken with some or all of the participants. As the program gets underway, the best facilitators know the audience because they watch for signs of interest (or boredom), physically walk among the crowd, and make themselves vulnerable. Fearless facilitators allow the audience to talk, interact, and become part of the experience. So, like our student Sho Yano, pause and reflect before you speak. Then, just as improv actors do, trust yourself to say "yes . . . and" rather than "yes . . . but."

When You Know More and They Came to Hear It

We once attended a workshop where the presenter had specific knowledge that the audience did not. They had come to listen, not to share or interact. Because he was the expert, they wanted his material and his wisdom. We watched the presenter give the microphone and a sheet of paper to an audience volunteer. He christened this person "the Voice of God" and asked him to read the twelve questions on the sheet one at a time. This volunteer, the presenter said, was to ensure that this Q&A section would take about forty minutes, which would leave plenty of time for the thirteenth question (which would be the most important of all). The volunteer was encouraged to keep the presenter on track by interrupting with the next question whenever the volunteer saw fit.

- The presenter authored the questions.
- The presenter knew the answers.
- The audience was ready to listen.
- The audience had a big incentive to stay for the thirteenth question!
- The volunteer kept the presenter on time.

The forty minutes sped by without any audience questions, and when completed, the audience was able to ask questions. A few people raised their hands, but mostly everybody wanted to know what Number 13 was going to be!

The presenter was able to relax. In fact, he just sat on the stage as he was "interviewed." The format was utter genius! The fearless facilitator knows how to be unpredictably interesting to foster a deeper connection with the people in front of him or her. Our world of instruction, teaching, and training is often reduced to one person talking and others listening (or acting as if they are). We expect learning to happen, but we often see nodding heads, not from their inner "yes" but from their inner "Is it over yet?" As such, the audience acts as if they are learning, when in fact they may not be learning at all, simply listening with more or less interest.

As you know, Kevin specifically asks that his presentation venues have no tables. He asks only for moveable chairs, often putting the audience in random, changing groups of two and three for short, focused discussions with his "lecturettes" punctuating the flow. More than one attendee often remarks, "This was a great lecture!" They didn't even have the words to describe the experience beyond what they have grown to know, a lecture! If they'd known they'd say, "Nice facilitation!"

A point of clarification is due here: facilitation does not always mean that the audience is talking to one another or engaged in an activity. Good facilitation means that the presenter made it easy for the audience to "get it."

For example, another presenter we know uses no PowerPoint whatsoever. Instead, she uses pre-printed flip charts that decorate the room with quotes, words, bullet points, and designs. She then refers to each sheet as she goes through her presentation. Her students think these sheets are visual aids; she knows they are her notes! It keeps her, and her students, on track!

When You Need to (and Should) Keep Emotion at Bay

A national radio program host was interviewing a historical researcher about his latest book on the history and beliefs of the Mormon church. He answered each question with precision, without bias, and lacking personal emotion. His answers conveyed the emotions of the members of the church but not his own emotion. Halfway through the interview, the host asked if he, the author, was a Mormon. "Yes," he said. The host then asked if being both a member and an objective historian and researcher were at odds with each other. He admitted to the tension, then said that his scholarly work was important to him, but so was his faith. His research, he said, would only be truly useful if it could be seen as pure. Contrast that with another well-known author interviewed about his history of government. He answered the questions with authority, but when he spoke of each president, he imitated the man's voice. When asked direct questions about controversial issues, he gave out dogmatic answers. Underlying each answer was an attitude that conveyed he thought himself to be smart, wise, even better than the listeners.

Fearless facilitators evaluate each situation for the amount of emotion required. None sometimes makes you more.

You and I run the risk of actually being perceived as, or feeling as, if we are the smartest person in the room. As author Randy Gage suggests, "If you feel like you are the smartest person in the room, you need a new room!" Even kindergarten teachers know that they are not the smartest people in the room, for their little ones remind them of that each day. The fearless facilitator is the most inquiring person in the room . . . and lets the audience teach him or her!

"The best facilitator and moderator is the one they stop directing all the questions to."
—*Ken Johnson, PharmD, DuraTherapeutics*

When You Can't Think and Hit at the Same Time

We've spoken frequently about the importance of mingling and merging with the audience as you facilitate. When you're out among them, however, you may not always receive the responses for which you had hoped or that you had expected. Some may be angry, doubtful, childish, inappropriate, or self-serving. To the beginning facilitator, this can be daunting, but to the veteran, this is when the fun begins. When you don't have a lot of time to think of the perfect response to the difficult comment, tell yourself to just "go with it." As Yogi Berra once said, "You can't think and hit at the same time." Without thinking too hard, you can often hit the home run by "going with your gut" or trusting your ability to think on your feet. There's no time to weigh the pros and cons. Try to break the habit of second-guessing what your "correct" response should be. You can do this in any one of the following ways:

- Respond with encouraging, neutral questions such as, "That's interesting. How did you arrive at that?" or " Hmm . . . how does that work for you?" Become so comfortable with these two questions that they are readily retrievable—an integral part of your facilitator "script."

- Respond with outrageous humor that the commentator would never expect, such as "What? Are you nuts?" or "Wow, have you been tracking with us today at all?" To use this technique, you must absolutely establish early on that you have a sense of humor. Have a smile on your face and a twinkle in your eye as you deliver the outrageous. Caution: this is not to be used with all groups!

- Respond by listening carefully, then using the subtle "Tag and add . . ." technique (described in the previous chapter), where you simply restate a portion of the response. For example, imagine you're leading a session for customer service call center managers; in the discussion a participant says, "We've heard this same stuff over and over, and when I tell my team about it, they just laugh." Your "tag and add" response would then be "They laugh?" (You are simply repeating selected words.) This encourages the participant to comment further; for example, he or she may say, "Yeah, they find it hilarious that we expect them to solve every customer call problem in three minutes." Now you have uncovered the key issue, which is the three-minute time limit for call operators and managers' challenges to motivate and reinforce such a limit.

  Think of a game of "catch." You are simply letting the other person know that you "caught" his or her words and are throwing them back, you hope so the person will catch your words as well and continue the "play." You can repeat the "tag and add" technique a few times before it begins to sound parrot-like or awkward.

Home Run!

When all the bases are loaded and the pressure is on, the home run becomes the "grand slam." There are times when we're facilitating when everything just clicks. The team is playing well together and the goal of the program is being achieved beyond expectations. Those times—those grand slams or even just those home runs—are so invigorating and motivating to those of us who have committed to being pros at getting people talking. We glow in the appreciation of the group for a meaningful experience, whether it is a major conference or a weekly meeting.

Experience teaches us that those glowing times will come if we can patiently "go with it" during the unexpected, difficult, and even demoralizing ones. Like a coach in the Olympics watching her gymnasts, there comes a time when it is up to the athlete; the coach can only watch and cheer. This may happen to you as well. Your audience member says something so well, so clearly, so helpfully that all you can do is step back and appreciate. Be careful here. Many presenters and facilitators think this is the time for them to take back the microphone and add their part. Let the athlete do his or her job alone!

Coach's Comments

- It sounds like a great deal of this relies on my instinct, my in-the-moment-ness of what is happening. How do I prepare for that?

It does rely on your active presence. We have found that there are at least three things that can prepare you better than anything else:

1. Preparation of your material in conjunction with who is coming to this event. The more you know the audience, the better prepared you will be. By this we don't just mean the people in the audience, but we mean why they are coming, what they want from coming, what their needs and desires are. Therefore, if this is a group you see every day, it is important not to assume that you "know" them. Their agenda for today may not be your agenda for today.

2. The fearless facilitator meets each audience as if it is an entirely new group of people, and while doing so builds upon the foundations of connections that he or she has built in the past.

3. Survey those coming with one simple question: "When we fin-
    ish today, what do you want from today's meeting, from my
    presentation, that would help you the most?" Simply asking
    the question will put you miles ahead; the answer will keep you
    there. Be very open to the audience's experience. Be ever watch-
    ful for how the audience is responding to the presenter who
    precedes you, and how they seem to be, how they are with you.

4. Be on the lookout for engagement. Cyndi and Kevin teach at
    Columbia College, the largest performing arts school in the
    United States. They teach actors and actresses a required class
    called "Speaking Out." Their students therefore are wildly cre-
    ative. It is akin to what it must be like backstage at "Saturday
    Night Live" with jokes, one-liners, fast reactions, mimics, and
    imitations abounding at every class. If we tried to keep up
    with the creativity of our students, we'd be lost. Instead, we
    know our job is to begin it, to initiate, and to engage. It no
    longer is about us, but about them.

The fearless facilitator aims first to be useful and rarely seeks perfection. Very good facilitators want to be the grease that helps the
machine work at its best. This means that you are not the star, they are!

- Is it ever appropriate to simply discipline or call out someone
  who gives an inappropriate response?

Absolutely, as the facilitator is expected to engage in crowd control,
so a response in an even tone is appropriate when a participant's question or comment is not. Examples may be, "I'm not going to allow or
promote that discussion here" or "I can see you have strong feelings;
we just can't air them in this format." Humor is good if the situation
warrants it and you've established yourself as a facilitator who has a
sense of humor. For example, "Where in the world did you come up
with that idea?" (SMILE) or "I've been hoping for just that response all
day" (SMILE) are lighter ways of dealing with someone's poor choices.
Don't ever let the bad apple spoil the bunch.

Nine

It's About the Audience, First and Always, in All Ways!

"I serve as the president of a state membership organization, and have always had a difficult time getting my board members to volunteer to do the work that we all agree needs to be done. When I've asked questions about our goals for the year, I've been met with silence. But when I split them into small groups, the whole dynamic changed. It was 7:15 a.m. and they were talking louder than I've heard in years! They were contributing, volunteering, and encouraging one another. Facilitation brought our group together. What a great thing to have happen at my board meeting when we all came together!"

—*Terry Sheeler, President, National Federation of the Blind of Arkansas*

- Know your audience in order to connect successfully.

- Adapt your knowledge and expertise to the group.

- Beware of receiving (or giving) too much information and advice.

How often do you research the audience first? Many professionals head to the computer to begin writing or fine-tuning their notes, adjusting their PowerPoint, or simply heightening their anxiety. While it can be productive to begin thinking about your content early on, it can be counterproductive to deliver content that isn't customized to the crowd.

Consider yourself as the audience member. How do you want your presenter to know you? Even if you are leading the meeting you lead every week for the same team, you will benefit from doing your homework.

- Text, call, or e-mail key players—especially your "problem folks" who are likely to object, conflict, or oppose—beforehand to collect their thoughts on a controversial or even an easy subject.

- Send out a short survey to obtain their reactions to a change you're proposing.

- Do what the politicians do: "leak" some information, take them into your confidence, or simply ask them point-blank for their thoughts, concerns, or even their support.

It's much better to do this ahead of the meeting than have them decide to do it during the meeting!

The fearless facilitator considers audience survey as the essential first step.

A Question for the Coach

I would love any ideas you may have regarding the opening day with my staff. We will meet from 8:30 to 10:30 a.m. in the auditorium with an audience of 140 staff members, including teachers, teacher assistants, speech therapists, counselors, business office staff, facilities, and grounds workers, and others. We typically have a PowerPoint presentation, and I often show a media piece connected with the theme. Even though we meet in the auditorium, we still can divide into small groups or move around.

Two years ago, we created some powerful guiding documents that include a new mission statement, vision statement, bilingual belief statements, organizational values, and a strategic plan. Our board of trustees would like me to review these with all staff at the beginning of each year.

If you have any creative ideas I could use for revisiting these guiding documents, without boring everyone to tears, it would be GREAT.

The Coach Advises

How about a kickoff quiz game, similar to trivia night at your neighborhood pub. Ask questions centered on some fun facts about staff members' vacations, childhoods, and special talents. Call some of your "characters" and your "big personalities" from every department, and include questions about them. Intersperse these fun questions with ones about your mission, vision statements, and strategic plan. You could also have some "odd" school budget items, such as how many French fries were consumed last year or how many red pens were ordered.

During the meat of the program, you could interview a board member on stage, an alumnus, or a current student. Intersperse the session with rotating groups of two or three, tasked to answer focus questions that seek positive responses.

Finish it off with some media, perhaps highlighting the school and its people. Audiences such as this love to see pictures of themselves and their co-workers. Take this year to accumulate more pictures and use them on a slide show.

Even if you are in an auditorium with fixed seats, this can be a fully interactive program!

And, oh yes, get off the stage from time to time and wander the aisles!

What a Ninety-One-Year-Old Knows

Cyndi's father lived for a while in a small nursing home where the staff did its best to entertain the residents with various local performers, musicians, and speakers. Most of these events were met with considerable interest, but none were as well attended as Bingo, which was always scheduled after the entertainment while the residents were already together. Once, when she and her father were conversing about the speakers, she asked if he enjoyed them. His reply was, "You know they go on and on; we don't like it when they take up our Bingo time."

This candid reaction from a ninety-one-year-old is an honest reminder to all of us that even nursing home audiences have likes, dislikes, and priorities. So, if you present to elderly audiences, you have some audience research to do! For example, experienced nursing home presenters and facilitators know:

- Most elderly people like routines and patterns.

- Many have short attention spans and are easily distracted.

- Some may make inappropriate comments or be extremely non-participative.

- Many find joy in rhythm and music.

To prepare for this audience, the fearless facilitator asks questions such as these:

- What is the average age and situation of most of the residents?

- Will most be in wheelchairs?

- What activities will occur before and after my presentation?

- How likely are they to be involved?

- Is there an incentive I can provide to involve them or spur their interest (a piece of candy, a coupon, or a toy)?

- Is there a leader in the group who will help me start the discussion?

- What's my time frame? How long is too long?

- Are they able to be interactive with hand-raising or short replies?

- Is a handout helpful or distracting?

- Should I incorporate some type of music?

Yes, this is a true story . . . and it is a powerful metaphor for every audience! How many times has a presenter interfered with what you considered to be your "Bingo time," whether that is lunch, alone time, e-mail, or cocktail hour?

The important first step to success for any facilitator is taking the time to prepare and ask questions, always ending with: "Is there anything else about this audience that you know that I do *not* know that would make this an engaging presentation?" Another good one—especially for a professional audience—is: "What do you think the other attendees (besides you) need to know?" When you ask individual attendees what they think the other audience members should know, you will often find out what that person needs but is reticent to speak about; you will discover the politics involved; and certainly you'll find out the emotional piece that is so important.

The fearless facilitator knows how to dialogue with individual audience members to gather great information beforehand.

What a Professional Magician Knows

Dennis DeBondt is a life-long professional magician with a successful business in both the corporate and children's entertainment arenas. Here's a review of his work from *Chicago* magazine: "The deft prestidigitation of Dennis DeBondt—his card tricks, mentalism, and stylish magic shtick—is complemented by a biting sense of humor. Fortune 500 CEOs and four-year-old kids alike respond with the same blend of incredulity, laughter, and appreciation—even jaded parents drop their jaws when DeBondt pulls a playing card, chosen at random by a member of the audience, out of his shoe."

Dennis has learned over the years that he doesn't need a minutia of information about either companies or kids. Rather than asking his clients what to do with respect to involving them, he instead asks what not to do. As he puts it, "I just need to know the one thread on the sweater that might unravel the whole thing if I pull it." Normally, Dennis works with seamless skill involving his audiences, knowing whom to ask to volunteer and whom to avoid, based on the information his client has given him. But he recalls he once made a faux pas, for which he ended up apologizing for years afterward. It was during a show for a corporate client who told him in advance to select anyone as a volunteer except Liz. "DON'T ASK LIZ," the client said. But that evening, for some reason, he went on "auto-pilot" and got to the last trick, where he usually asks a woman to help him, looked out, saw only one woman, and asked her to come forth. It was Liz! As the company's owner, she was not too happy about it. Dennis adds, "I think they hire me back each year to hear me apologize again. Each year the apology gets more elaborate. Last year I brought flowers!"

Dennis likens a great magic presentation to jazz: know the beginning and the end, and be ready to improvise a lot along the way. If only all of us could use magic and humor and fun in all of our presentations!

The fearless facilitator has a planned beginning and ending and is ready to improvise a lot in between.

What an Eighth-Grade Teacher Knows

Jane Sweeney, a finalist in the "Golden Apple" teaching excellence awards and career-long elementary school teacher, most often has taught pre-teens and eighth graders. Teachers by trade are usually quite good at involving their students in the lesson with hands-on activities that make it come to life. But adolescents can be especially challenging to excite about a topic. Jane advises, "I do know that if you can involve a class with decision making about anything they are involved with, their attitude about everything in class is better. For example, recently we had to decide how our class would participate in the school-wide volleyball game. Just asking them what they think is a great way to get twelve-year-olds 'in your palm.'"

Cyndi was once asked to talk about being a professional speaker for an eighth-grade career day at her children's school. Equipped with questions and examples, she thought she had a nice interactive program until the teacher interrupted in the middle of her talk. She suggested that Cyndi have a student volunteer speak impromptu in front of the group and then coach him or her on the spot. Hands went up as students readily volunteered (something Cyndi never expected) and the "career day talk" became less a talk and more an improvisational experience! The session ended with the class wanting more.

Most audiences are like eighth graders, for they want an experience. While it may not entail on-the-spot volunteering, the experience that they're seeking typically helps them enrich their work and their lives.

The fearless facilitator knows that when the audience is involved in the answer or solution, they are always more energized and committed to the outcome.

What Engineers Know

Typically, engineers are not an easy crowd to facilitate. Logical and methodical by nature, most engineers focus on the facts, processes, and results of a project presentation, caring less about being engaged or entertained. Or at least that is the myth!

That generalization, as Cyndi learned, is not always accurate: Her nephew, Leon, a young engineer at an international manufacturing firm, shared his first presentation experience at the firm, "I gave a presentation to the entire R&D division . . . more than 120 senior engineers and managers. I was volunteered by my boss to present his slides, which covered a big, costly project. I asked him if I could include my own flair and comedy and he agreed. I added quite a few jokes and joke slides and had the whole auditorium rolling. At the end I tied the jokes into the product theme with a 'failure is not an option' flair. Afterward, numerous section leaders came up to me to say what a good presenter I was. Personally, I think I barely pulled it off, but I guess the trick is to keep the audience engaged and to project confidence."

If your ego is up for it, you can also try what Kevin has found useful on his two-day retreats. Ask the group at periodic times to rate something on a scale of 1 to 10, where 10 is best, and to do so out loud. He usually brings everyone into a circle (no tables, of course!), pulls them closer together, and then says, "Let's see where all of you are so far with regard to getting what you need from this meeting. On a scale of 1 to 10, where 10 means you are highly satisfied with your learning and your insights, the value of this meeting, give us a number as I point to you. I'll only ask for the number, no explanation yet. Remember, I have no ego here! This is just about what value you are getting so far." Then Kevin points to one after another and the members call out a number. Some are 10s, some are 4s! Then he says, "Get into groups of three and discuss this: What would it take for you to raise your score just two points? What would need to change about us, and what needs to change about you?"

This not only gives Kevin a quick summary of how things are going, but it gives all individuals a goal to strive for that is ultimately about them and their involvement and less focused on others . . . or Kevin!

Cautions Using Humor

Remember that, although audiences like humor, you have to be careful about "telling jokes." Unless you are very, very good, proceed with caution. A funny story will often work, while jokes will not be as effective. Natural humor that comes from the audience is very appreciated, yet making fun of an audience member is very dangerous and could be interpreted as disrespectful. Allowing spontaneous contributions is a lot of fun, although planting responses in the audience ahead of time is risky.

Using cartoons in your PowerPoint slide deck can be met with mixed reactions! Here is a trick: remove the words. Just show the cartoon and ask, "What do you think the caption is?" Take their suggestions and then, and only then, show the cartoon with the caption. When you do, make sure you put the caption in LARGE print so that it is easily read. And, of course, one person's definition of funny is another person's definition of weird!

Connection Is Never Perfection

Successful audience connection results from experience, preparation, and, yes, lots of trial and error. Even though you've done your research and thought it through, you will never know exactly what the response will be to your attempt to engage and involve until you try it. The element of surprise is also the fun of facilitation. As you gain experience with certain types of participants based on their work, level of expertise, and industry, you can predict more accurately what they may do and say. We continue to compare notes on our latest clients to help each other prepare and adapt for the next ones. We encourage you to find others who will honestly share their experiences with audiences that you will address in the future. Do so right away and collect information before you desperately need it. This will greatly help you when your time comes to address the same group.

Connection will begin with you, however. Your engagement, your smile, your closeness to the audience, as well as your ability to greet the participants, are all ordinary and exceptionally vital ways to connect. They are also the very things that we forget to do routinely, intentionally, and professionally every time. While audiences are different, even with our very same material, it is never the audience's fault when things don't go so well. Our job is to adapt, not theirs. You will hear presenters and entertainers alike say afterward: "Tough crowd, tough crowd," when in fact what they need to say to themselves is: "What should I consider doing differently next time?"

The famous TV host Johnny Carson from "The Tonight Show," even after thirty years, was said to review the show from the night before for hints at how to make that night's show even better. This is professionalism at its best. Even someone as talented and famous as Johnny knew that the audience was the ultimate arbiter of his talent.

> The fearless facilitator knows that perfection every time is impossible, but self-critique and future change is very possible.

What the Professional Comedian Knows

Ken Sevara is a veteran comedian, radio host, and speaker. Ken's impressive background includes performances on national television and sharing the stage with Jerry Seinfeld, Jay Leno, Bill Murray, Richard Pryor, and George Carlin. Ken revealed his tips on the importance of the audience: "The main way I can tell if an audience is going to be great or not is the energy before the show. I walk in the room and I listen. The volume level tells you whether the energy is there; I can tell if I am going to have to work to get the audience immediately. If the energy is low, I know I've got some work cut out for me. Your volume and energy are important. You've got to bring them up to your level. Get their energy up!"

When asked about handling difficult comments and people, Ken says, "If you're a quarterback, you're gonna get sacked. It's no different in comedy. If you tell a joke that typically works, and for some reason it doesn't, (a) you didn't deliver it right or (b) you've got a tough crowd. Some people say there are no bad audiences. I disagree. There are very bad audiences. It's your job to really stay on them. Hopefully, if a joke doesn't work, you've got enough to bring them back. Jay Leno told me personally, 'The secret is in the editing. Only do the lines that are certain.' Develop a rhythm or cadence and build the laughs as closely as you can. Elayne Boosler also advised me to edit. There was not an ounce of fat in Elayne Boosler's act. She would write out every line; she would use an economy of words. She advised me to get to the punch line.

"A comedian also learns about handling audiences by watching. We would sit in the back of the Comedy Store main room in Los Angeles, watching the greats like Robin Williams, David Lettermen, and Richard Pryor work the mike, talk to the crowd, the timing, and the attitudes they took.

"It's always important that you don't put the audience down. Comedy is always based on the audience feeling they're superior to you. You never want to come off as some sort of elitist. Don't go into a small town and pull off a big city attitude. I want them to come along with me; I don't want to act like I'm superior to them. The other thing: enjoy yourself. Buddy Hackett told me, 'If you go up there thinking of yourself, for example, "Am I looking OK? Am I feeling Ok?" you're forgetting why you're up there.' You're up there to make people happy and to make people smile."

Five Things to Learn from the Comedian

- Get among them beforehand and sense their energy level.

- With a tough crowd, the secret is editing; choose your most certain material.

- Watch other great facilitators and "steal" their techniques.

- Don't ever put the audience down.

- Have fun!

Audiences Will React Differently to the Same Story

We can appreciate the experiences of the professional comedian who can tell the same joke to many different crowds with many different reactions. The real pro takes it in stride and keeps moving. The fearless facilitator edits and adapts the story for next time and tries again.

To introduce a presentation on the topic of influence, Cyndi tells a story about sitting next to a beauty queen miniature dachshund named "Tootsie" on a four-hour flight to Los Angeles. The story unfolds as Cyndi, who was in the middle seat, gets to know Tootsie and her owner, seventy-two-year-old Pearl, who is quite an outgoing character. When Cyndi returns home, she is surprised to find a letter from Pearl, letting her know the results of the American Kennel Club contest they were heading to: Tootsie took a second and third place to the winning breed, a standard dachshund, which is hard for the miniature to beat.

After sharing the story, Cyndi asks the audience to choose the "character" they relate to most and why. She also reminds them to consider the theme of influence, "Who had the most influence?" or "What is the lesson on influence in the story?" The reactions she receives vary greatly depending on the type of group.

- Women's groups typically buzz with ideas immediately after she fields the question. Their responses are funny; most often they relate to Pearl, but also to Tootsie.

- Sales groups of mixed gender, healthcare providers, and insurance people also have fun with the questions and arrive at creative answers very quickly.

- On the other hand, financial managers and engineers are slower to respond; their answers are less creative and almost never funny. With these audiences, Cyndi has learned to facilitate more closely by probing with more questions to help their thinking. For example, "Do you ever feel stuck in the middle seat when you attempt to influence?" "Are you cheerleaders for your information, as was Pearl?"

Notice here that telling the story is one thing; "facilitating" the story is quite another. Telling will inform; facilitating will involve. Telling will entertain; facilitating will provide a memorable experience. Telling is OK; facilitating is A-OK!

After telling the story, the fearless facilitator facilitates the story.

Avoid Death by Committee

The old adage, "Too many cooks spoil the broth," holds true for planning a successful audience response. While preparation is certainly important, be careful of trying to please too many people; you'll end up going into a program with too much information and too many goals. The final "broth" will be diluted to a watery, tasteless mess.

Cyndi recalls a time when she was working with a committee of six advisors on a high-level corporate team to plan an international meeting presentation. What began as an exciting opportunity to plug in the perspective of the highest levels and experience ended in "death by committee." All their ideas seemed valid: using customized case studies, sharing best practices, mingling groups that were often in competition for resources, and more. Against her better judgment, she attempted most of them with a group that was too large in a room that was too large. The result was a discussion of over-simplistic generalities, rather than the applicable action steps that audiences appreciate.

In general, beware of too much advice on what to do and not to do. Certainly, get your audience information from a variety of sources, but when it comes down to it, trust your own education, experience, and instincts as you make final decisions about format and engagement. More than three thousand speakers are members of the National Speakers Association, and each facilitates his or her audiences differently. They also know that one audience may love their style and another may dislike it. The veterans know that audience preparation is very important, and they also learn quickly not to trust one person's opinion.

Rather than seek any advice on "how" to speak to the audience, redirect your inquiry to the outcomes the audience desires. You are the surgeon, and they are the patients. The patients tell what hurts, they say how they want to feel better, and the surgeon knows how to make that happen. You are the surgeon!

Fearless facilitators carefully avoid too many opinions on how to do the meeting, instead agreeing on the desired outcomes with the client before the meeting.

Audience Soliloquy (Poem)

Columbia College Chicago theatre student Georgia Gove wrote the impressive piece below as her final presentation in our "Speaking Out" class. She eloquently captures the spirit of this chapter.

The Audience
By Georgia Gove (12/16/11)

It is you that makes my Talk wonderful.

I, the Speaker, pale before you.

The Talk too pales before your incredible power.

Well-written words are just that;

They are good on paper, but they end there.

It is the Audience that determines the greatness of words;

They will see that I fail if my words they don't like.

Shakespeare, JFK, Lewis CK:

These men would be nothing without their audience.

They judge my Talk,

They laugh or they cry,

Or they simply refuse to react

And they reject the words I wrote.

My audience is my inspiration.

My audience is my catalyst.

For without the audience, no Talk would there be.

I, the Speaker, cannot write a Talk for myself

Without the Audience,

What need have I to write a Talk?

The Talk, affected by the audience

Acquires a new light, a new feeling.

The audience crackles with energy.

The energy they have I use

To make my Talk better,

To make me a better Speaker.

If they have bad energy,

My energy will too be low.

If they have good energy,

My energy will be great also.

To make my Talk energized,

I feed off the liveliness of the audience.

The Talk may be great

For I wrote it to be perfect,

But it is the Audience that reacts to the words I write,

Not I, the Speaker, who performs it.

They may think what I wrote is not funny in the least,

They may think what I wrote is hilarious.

What I thought they would think meaningful,

My audience may think a travesty.

Yet, they could think funny and meaningful

Something I thought of as nothing much.

How well I write the Talk may not matter,

The Audience reacts as they will.

The Audience can make a Speaker great,

Or they can keep the Speaker from greatness.

The Talk is made for them,

And without the Audience, it wouldn't exist.

Ten

Yikes! A Whole Room Full of . . .

"If you have to choose between people remembering what you say and that feeling that they get from you, you're far better off if they forget what you said and remember that feeling."

—*Fredric K. Schroeder, Ph.D., former commissioner, U.S. Department of Education, Rehabilitation Services Administration*

- Predict the challenges you will experience as a fearless facilitator.

- Predicting lessens the chances of things happening; it also prepares you for what will surely happen.

- Develop special facilitation strategies for audiences of one type: volunteers, one gender, culture, job role, age group, and professional introverts!

- Understand the psychology of the group and you will be better able to serve them, and shield yourself!

- Adapt when you find that your expertise is not what the audience came to hear. While we advocate being transformational, a few transactional techniques can save you.

- When death, discouragement, and disease threaten your world with them, learn to never run out of tricks when the tried-and-true techniques stop working effectively.

One of the hallmarks of fearless facilitation is your own ability to "make it easier" for yourself. Throughout this book we have encouraged you to not only think of yourself as a presenter to a large group, but to engage your presence with others in many ways. Like it or not, from the moment you wake up until you shut out the lights at night, your work, time, and life are about facilitating yourself and others to get to the next right step in the best way.

We have encouraged you to capture your essence in your smile and your connectivity with others:

- From your pre-presentation meet and greet

- To the way you use your lively eye contact in an intentional way as others ask you questions

- To how you move away from the lectern or the front of the room and mix and mingle yourself with each and every audience

- To allowing the audience to answer questions directed at you

- To using the uniqueness of each audience member whether former military, Eagle scouts, world travelers, or studying the trapeze; seek and know something about this specialness

- To how you begin, how you weigh in, and how you bid them a fond farewell; all of these more fully engage your presence for them, for you, and for the world

When Times Go Less Well Than Planned

Fearless facilitators learn to avoid the "deer in the headlights" look, which some presenters feel when the audience takes on a strong presence or attitude. If you haven't already had the experience, the time will come when you face an audience and feel like a foreigner. Perhaps they are there for one thing and you thought for another. Robert Louis Stevenson said, "There are no foreign lands, only the visitor is foreign." So, too, here: when we feel "foreign" our work is to take an assertive step back mentally. Assertive in the sense that we don't shrink from the task, step back in the sense that we listen with our eyes and our ears, that we allow them to talk to one another, perhaps set a revised agenda with them, have them form small groups, move to the flip charts around the room (yes, the flip chart is your friend!), and allow them to accomplish a task together.

People and Groups Who Exhibit Predictable Challenges

Here are just a few challenges that you will likely see as soon as you begin implementing the mindset of a fearless facilitator. There is no real way to prepare a script for these times. Instead, prepare a mindset that you want the audience to understand and implement. Learn to rely on your in-the-moment skills that we discussed in Chapter Eight.

You must first trust the audience before they will return the favor. Horse whisperers, trainers who use gentle techniques to work with the horse rather than any attempt to "break" the horse, know that the key in this endeavor is to establish trust. This is done best when we find ways to exhibit not only nonthreatening behavior, but also when we are fully aware that trust is given as well as perceived, granted as well as offered, initiated as well as anticipated. When a horse whisperer is at work, there is no fear on the part of the trainer, no anticipation of danger, only structured permission. As the horse circles the trainer it is allowed to move freely with a long lead, ever repeating a circle that builds trust and reliance: this human is no threat!

When you trust the audience, they will feel trusted. When you don't, watch out! It is extremely easy to mistakenly over-control an audience.

Imagine how a wedding planner might easily mistake giggling and loud voices before the church rehearsal as non-cooperation when it instead stems from excitement. The planner yelling, "Shut up!" to the friends and family would definitely qualify as over-controlling.

We prefer a different technique to quiet any crowd, large or small. In your typical volume and tone, ideally with a microphone but not required, say, "If you can hear me, please raise your hand" and keep yours raised. Then repeat it no more than two or three times. We've found that this quiets the savage beast and is a gentle way to bring everyone back to focus. Likewise:

- It is very, very easy to assume wrongly based on legitimate observation.
- Blank faces do not always mean boredom.
- Disagreement is not always a reflection on you.
- Conflict between opposing groups is not always bad.

You just have to establish some ground rules and be the one to gently enforce them. Some facilitators worry so much about their message getting out that they override the audience.

Remember, their message, their learning, their memories supersede yours! When you find yourself in the midst of this quandary, establish some discipline within yourself to be very careful to:

- Not over-talk
- Rely on open questions that genuinely reflect your natural curiosity
- Move physically closer to those who speak
- Paraphrase the daylights out of them!
- Use the flip chart to show that you understand and to help others draw connections between ideas

We've seen facilitators spar and war with an audience.

Some time ago, our Senators and Congressmen returned home after a contentious political season to some "town hall" meetings (a political friend called them "town hell" meetings!). As we watched our politicians, we noticed some decided to debate and battle those in attendance, essentially fighting with their customers. Others had a bewildered and "moose in the headlights" look. Still others went silent, looked for the chief of staff to get them out of there, or just cut the meeting short.

The smart ones facilitated. Those who moved in close to the audience understood, just as martial arts practitioners do, that others cannot hurt you, or will hurt you less, if you are close to them. Other smart ones continued to look both for common ground and give appreciation for constituents' attendance through their body language, words, and facial expressions.

The wise ones refused to become targets and rather became the chef stirring the pot of ingredients. As Dr. Michael Popkin from Georgia suggests so well, "We may not always get our way, but we do want our say."

Some simply give up in the face of what looks like a negative onslaught from a highly partisan crowd: never, ever give up.

Our experience is that, even though some will not like you, others will; some will disparage your message, others will be transformed by it; and still, while some will leave in disgust, others will be elated.

It is the nature of the audience beast to be multi-dimensional. You'll have to trust us on this one. Alfred Adler, the great Viennese psychiatrist from the early 1900s, remarked: "Alles kan immer ander sein." (Everything can always be otherwise!)

And by the way, you won't always receive perfect 10s on your evaluations. One colleague says that he throws out the top 10 percent of his evaluations, because "they will love me no matter what." Similarly, he pitches the bottom 10 percent because "They really will never like me!" He continued, "The truth lies in the middle. If only we will be aware and listen."

Of course, another option is not to read the evaluations at all! One top speaker we know has this rule so that his sensitivities are not subjected to his own perfectionism. (We think he'd learn a good amount if he got out of his own way.)

This high level of trust comes with simply doing it more and more each time. It is an attitude, an approach, and a mindset that is subtle but will serve you very well. Over-controlling, excessively worried, approval-seeking presenters and facilitators never experience a profound mutuality with an audience.

Your new approach to meetings will, at first, create a state of natural confusion, and that is OK. You'll need to engage, connect, and maintain momentum with others, even when it appears they seem disinterested in doing so. Many times we are desperately looking for approval from the audience as we speak. This is a mistake of the first order. It is akin to a pilot in trouble asking the passengers, "What do you think I should do?" Your leadership is vital, even if the audience is staring blankly at you. Remember, you don't have access to some of their distracting thoughts, unless you fearlessly facilitate.

Kevin was speaking to a retinal surgeon recently who had just come back from some speaker training for women physicians. He gave her a copy of our book, *Speak Up: A Woman's Guide to Presenting Like a Pro*, and she pointed to the title and said excitedly, "This is what they told us to do!" Then she continued, indicating that this was difficult because these were not always her meetings. Kevin cautioned, "When you speak, if only for a moment or two, it is your meeting." This is the mindset you must always have, for the audience wants your structure, your leadership, and your initiative.

The wedding planner we referred to earlier began the rehearsal with the following words: "Does anyone have any idea how we should do this?" Yikes! You can imagine the chaos that followed. Protocol be damned, everyone had his or her own spin on who goes where and what is what! Later she wisely said, "OK everyone, I'm the planner and here is what we are going to do!" All laughed good-naturedly as she took back her rightful role, her rightful power.

While a democratic approach seeking input is a good thing in some situations, it certainly is not in wedding rehearsal planning, airplane emergencies, or highly task-driven meetings of all sorts. Remember, this is your meeting.

Would You Want to Perform Here?

Take a look at the audience the next time you're in attendance and listening (a play, comedy club, or pastor's sermon). Would you want to be in front of them?

Actors, speakers, and pastors have told us that they focus 50 percent of their attention on their biggest fans in the audience (maybe that guy in the front row who thinks every joke is the funniest one of the night) to keep their excitement level high. They focus the other 50 percent on connecting with the blank stares. The key here is that the skilled professionals (and you as a fearless facilitator are one) monitor but do not dwell only on the blank stares. Seek out those who are loving you and, while not exclusively playing to them, know that they are the backbone of your support and encouragement, and they may even be giving voice and glance to the more hidden thoughts and feelings of the quieter blank faces next to them.

Stay very aware of your "locus of control," the Latin "locus" is that place deep within yourself that allows you to come to awareness. Feeling, thinking, and acting independently are key in directing the focus of your meeting as a fearless facilitator. Take care not to give this place of control away to others. You, too, can and should always be prepared to take the next right step. As you have read so far, this is as much a mental process on your part as it is a concrete one.

Kevin has a habit of watching movies on airplanes without the sound. The plot for him is not important; he observes the actors.

Of course, none of this is easy! Some of it is downright hard to do, especially on a consistent basis. We've noticed that it is one thing to bring our expertise to an audience, but it is quite another to engage them in a rigorous and engaging dialogue. It is one thing to be the parent, and quite another to listen to your adolescent as if he or she had something important to say! (They often do!) It is one thing to "know"; quite another to "do." As the fearless facilitator, allow for divergent opinions, all the while knowing that this is your meeting that they are attending and in which they are co-collaborating with you. Provide structure; just don't be too structured.

Groups of men and women often react differently to the same material. In our experience, men appreciate all that is clear, simple, and direct, especially when presented in a visually stimulating and provocative way, with less group interaction. Women, on the other hand, appreciate time to process concepts with in partners or groups, as long as the point is relevant to their work. Women may be quieter in a large group, opening up considerably in smaller ones. Of course, there are exceptions to every rule!

So at the risk of you-know-what, here is your gender-neutral and gender-aggressive plan:

Mostly or All Male Audiences	Mostly or All Female
Assert without aggression	Understand without weakness
Concrete without the obvious	Subtle and deeper
Specific grouping directions	Enjoy individual responses
Redirect the loud guy	Watch for the non-verbals
Yes, sports analogies are OK	Psychology before sports
Prepare for sarcasm	Prepare for a disagreeing smile
Shorter attention span	The eyes will tell you the timing
Breaks will be taken liberally	Will return in fifteen minutes
Openly confrontational questions	Subtle confrontations
Like early endings	Like early endings

People Who Are Disconnected

The following techniques are more about your awareness than they are about changing yourself or your presentation because of the audience's vocation. When you see masterful presenters at work in difficult conditions with uncooperative or with unresponsive audiences, what they are really doing is tweaking what they had planned to do in almost unnoticeable ways.

When You Find That Your Opinion Is in the Minority

Your first reaction may be to . . . react! Instead, listen as you present, being careful not to raise your voice, feel any pressure, or show any sign of frustration. Watch for the slightest head nods, the flicker of warmth from selected eyes, and even note when your audience takes notes. In short, you are listening, gathering intelligence, and presenting all at the same time. And then be assured of our style of government and culture, it is OK to be a minority, to hold the minority opinion, to be at the forefront of what will someday be a majority, and to be a voice crying out in the wilderness! The main thing is not to shrink. One thing we have learned from the ever-present talk-show format of constant news and opinion television shows is that she and he in the minority who step back into the shadows have lost. If you believe it, say it! And when you say it, never apologize (especially if you are a woman) and never dismiss the other (especially if you are a man).

Fearless facilitators remember that every majority opinion in our history was once a minority one, or it at least helped the majority win favor!

When the audience is quiet, remember that facilitation can exist with a silent, as well as spoken, dialogue. While you are attempting to gain influence, access their thinking, and direct their judgment, your best bet—by far—is to create a conversation, even only inside each audience member's mind. There will be plenty of time for spoken dialogue when you facilitate their talking to you, but be extremely vigilant in keeping them in your awareness as you make your case. The contrary behavior, however, to this skill is to ramble, to force, to go on and on and on, or even to wither. All of these elements focus on one's self.

The fearless facilitator focuses on the other in the context of himself or herself.

When Your Expertise and Skills Don't Match What the Audience Needs

Whether they are more or less advanced, don't let either intimidate you. Kevin has specialized in working with pharmaceutical teams for two decades, and he still barely understands the content of their meetings. In fact, when he is asked to sign a confidentiality agreement not to disclose what he hears, he often wants to ask for a stupidity agreement—one that will clarify that he has no aptitude to understand the scientific content! What he does know and why he is hired is for his presentation, facilitation, team leadership, and communication expertise—that which is hardly ever taught in pharmacy school. Smarter audiences, and those less so, are the same, for they relish the opportunity to talk with one another. The funny thing is that they learn regardless. We just have to make sure we get out of their way, don't compete, don't fake it, don't apologize, and don't try to cram. Rather, know who you are and what you know and why you are there.

"Single-focused" audiences who share the same gender, mindset, culture, depressed energy, anger, sadness, or hostility can teach you a thing or two. These kinds of audiences are the most likely to be disrespected and to feel disrespect. Their extreme nature sets them up for difference. Resist the temptation to internally segregate them from your more diverse or friendly audiences. Instead, increase your awareness and resolve to learn from them. Inquire, develop, and suspend judgment, wonder, and experiment instead of presenting only a single message.

We both teach communication courses at two very different universities: Columbia College Chicago, a communication arts school, and Loyola University, a Catholic university in the Jesuit tradition. We absolutely love both experiences and both student groups. The Columbia students tend to be artsy, edgy, trendy, and assertively nonconventional. The Loyola students tend to be polite, more quiet, respectful of the instructor's opinion, and conventional. Of course, there are exceptions, but this is what we've come to expect as we facilitate learning in both groups. The same story goes over differently; the same assignment elicits different concerns and questions; and the commitment to discussion depends on the topic. These young people serve to re-teach us the importance of audience awareness.

Fearless facilitators are ever aware that they must color their lecturettes to each audience's unique concerns, styles, and interests . . . always ready for unpredicted audience reactions.

When You Are Absolutely the Wrong Presenter for This Audience (and You and Everyone Else Know It)

Admit it! In the movie *Up in the Air*, George Clooney's character realizes that the speech he is giving is not the one that is in his heart. He leaves the stage. (Now, we never recommend leaving the stage!) But there are times when you know you are not a right fit for this audience, for this meeting, or for this message. Knowing what you know is important; knowing what you don't know is more so!

Sometimes, however, your bosses will ask you to fill in for them and you have to present material with which you are unfamiliar. So don't fake it. If you do, they will know and your reputation (not your boss's) will be in jeopardy.

Here's a more professional tactic than what Clooney's character did:

- Call the meeting to order and say, "Claire was double-scheduled today and asked me to take her place. She and I will send you her complete PowerPoint after today's meeting. What I'd like to do now is give us all an opportunity to discuss this material in more detail than we would normally have a chance to do. Therefore, as we begin, please get into groups of three, not with anyone who is sitting next to you."

- Give them time to organize and then say, "Regarding [the topic], what are your burning questions? What concerns you about [the topic] and what encourages you? I'll give you three or four minutes. Would each group please come up with a few questions? Ready? Go!"

- After a few minutes, bring them back together and write the questions on a flip chart. You now have a working agenda for the meeting. More importantly, you have something to take back to your boss, so that she is prepared for the questions that are most on the minds of those in attendance.

- For the rest of the meeting, you can talk about the questions that you can answer, enter into discussions about the others (always better in rotating small groups), and engage others in dialogue.

Don't they really want Claire though? Don't they really want a lecture? Don't they really want input, not discussion? In our experience the answer is a resounding "NO!"

Audiences say this because the experience—the rare chance of being able to talk to each other and to see that people in the group share the same questions—is just too rich of an experience to complain about. In fact, you, not Claire, may be invited back next time!

Sometimes, it is just the audience's fault. One professional speaker told us that at a dinner for an all-male group of salespeople, the audience became so drunk that they began a food fight during his introduction. They laughed, screamed, and applauded as he took the stage. He was very sober and knew that the prospects for his success, even on a minimal level, were next to zero. So he considered his response and said, "It's been great being with you all tonight. How about we retire to the bar for a nightcap?" They did and he left. Know how and when to leave!

Only One Person to Facilitate

There is no doubt that facilitating one-to-one is both easier and harder than in a group. Our job is to figure out what to do, mostly on the spot, by discerning the "next right move" to make, always focused on the other person. When we present from the podium (as one-to-one-hundred), we tend to think about our performance, the reception of the message, the outcomes for them, and the entire enterprise. When we are one-to-one, however, we run the danger of doing just the opposite: thinking about their behavior, focusing on our message, looking at the outcomes for us, and becoming bogged down in details. In short, we go from being someone who says "yes, and" to someone very ready to say "but. . . ." When that happens, we disconnect . . . and so does the other.

All that you have learned to this point can be directly applied to your one-to-one situations, too. Here are some strategies that you can use in every one-to-one meeting, whether there is strong emotion or you are merely (and importantly) leaving a voicemail. Be forewarned: all of this may appear to be quite simplistic. It is, yet well-meaning people like you and us violate it consistently every day!

Take the time to prepare mentally. Often, we forget this important step, regardless of what the interaction is going to be. You need not go into massive detail or even laborious time in this step, but it is vital that we think and consider what we want from this one-to-one interaction.

Then prepare dialogically and dyadically. Dialogue is conversation. A dyad is a couple. Dyadic conversations are not about you or me, for they are about "us"—an often-forgotten concept in our modern culture. Stop and listen to someone else's conversation. Frequently, these interactions boil down to a verbal tennis match, a "he said–she said–I said . . . and what did you say?" kind of conversation. How often have you heard a colleague say, "My kid won the soccer game last night!" only to hear someone else chime in with the likes of, "Oh, yeah? Both of my kids won their games last night!"

Give very considered thought to the fact that you have someone before you who wants to talk with you and wants you to focus on him or her.

As you speak, keep thinking before (responding) rather than after (reacting). Wise conversationalists are aware of what they need to do, not what they should have done. Of course, this is easier to say than to do, which is why this whole conversational facilitation is so difficult.

When we work with difference and conflict by using our first impulses, we are reacting not responding. Reaction is based on the other person's approach (you hit me, I hit you back . . . or I run!). The reactive approach takes your locus of control and puts it in the hands of the other person. Kevin's physician audiences often know more (or think they do!) about almost any topic that comes up. Even when Kevin is teaching his expertise that they signed up to learn, every one of them has an opinion, and some are devoted to not departing from it! Even knowing this, Kevin is often stuck with his inner reaction of wanting to "set them straight" or "tell them off" or the ultimate glory, them publicly admitting his superiority! (Not really!) But he does, we do, feel that inner visceral reaction when we are challenged. It is our reptilian brain, the amygdala, that is in charge at these moments. This part of our brain is our most primitive and it is the center of our fight-or-flight reactions. We need to engage the part of our brain that is our "figure it out" part. But rest assured, every one of us is put in this position from time to time.

Here are some quick tips to avoid when they engage the reptilian part of your brain!

- Avoid thinking that you will convince them against their will, especially publicly.

- Don't over-talk or try too quickly to move away from the topic being debated.

- Actively seek others' opinions by asking, "Anyone else feel a bit differently about this?"

- Definitely avoid using the words that will engage their amygdalas:

  - I disagree.

  - You're wrong.

- Your facts are weak.

- Who are you kidding?

- I doubt it.

- I totally disagree!

- Instead try these:

  - I hear you and I have a slightly different take on it. Would you like to hear it?

  - Thank you for that side of the issue. Is it OK with you if we hear from some others who might see things a bit differently still?

  - I have an idea; let's break up into groups of three and each group take a flip chart (remember, the flip chart is your friend!) and I'll give you twelve minutes (always give an unexpected number to be seen as different and creative) with your group to capture the debate graphically on your flip chart all sides of the debate.

- Others as needed:

  - I need your help.

  - Because . . .

  - The reason this is important is . . .

  - Can you give me an example of that?

  - Hearing you say that, I . . .

  - I want . . . need your help . . . because . . .

  - I hear you and I have a slightly different perspective.

  - You might be right.

  - What I appreciate about you is . . .

  - Thank you.

Alternatively, responding to difference involves more than a reaction, because it involves thought, feeling, and decision making. Adler once commented that we don't fight because we were angry. He said that we become angry in order to fight! This is not a fine-line distinction; it is a fundamental notion surrounding choice. While it may appear that feelings just come and go, Adler says that we use these feelings to achieve our goals.

Kevin had an audience member once who was very angry, perhaps because he had to attend a session he didn't want to attend. He was, however, the bane of this group's existence. He was itching for a fight. He wanted to engage. He was the equivalent of Mohammed Ali in the boxing ring inviting Kevin and anyone who would listen to come down for a few rounds. Luckily, Adler's disciple in America, Dr. Rudolf Dreikurs, also taught "Don't fight, don't give in." If we never approach the ring, the boxer can't land a punch!

Kevin took a risky move, but frankly the only one he had that would in any way overrule his very active, very seductive amygdala! Kevin said, "Jack, you are really angry about this." Silence. Then Jack said something that stunned Kevin and the crowd who knew him well. "I am angry. I'm an angry guy and everyone here knows it. I'm not proud of it, but I don't know what else to do when I think I'm right."

Yikes!

This then became a fearless facilitator's dream! "How many of you feel that way too sometimes?" Kevin said. Nearly every hand in the place went up! Guess what they all talked about next in small groups of three!

Kevin's inner thought was "Whew!"

The other cannot focus on you and your ideas if he or she is fighting with you, crowded with his or her own ideas, busy with something else on his or her mind, or—worse—sees you as of little value or relevance to his or her own goals. Like any fearless facilitator, you have to know when your content is just not ready for prime time. As with a presentation, especially a controversial or emotional one, there is a time and a place when the other is not mentally free enough to listen. To try to pack your "stuff" into them at that time is a losing effort.

Practice active listening.

Paraphrase, ask questions, employ empathy, be sincere, and help them understand that you understand. Simply doing well at this frees their minds, even if they are a mortal enemy. Robert McNamara, former Secretary of Defense under Presidents Kennedy and Johnson, warned: "Empathize with your enemy." Only then do you understand what is motivating them, what moves them forward, and what makes them make the decisions they have made and most likely will make.

What the Active Listener Says

- Really?
- What else?
- Wow!
- Tell me more about that!
- How did you decide to . . .?
- What was that like?

In Your Writing, Especially When You Need to Persuade

Empathize with your reader. Really work to get into the head of the person who is going to receive your e-mail, voicemail, card, or letter. What will he or she hear in your words from that perspective? One of our consulting colleagues swears she built her seven-digit business on ten thank-you notes per day, fifty per week, forty-eight weeks of the year. Her kids don't eat dinner till the tenth note is finished. How do you ignore a handwritten, not e-mailed, thank-you note? In and of itself the thank-you note (handwritten, not e-mailed!) is empathy and affirmation on steroids!

Gaining Traction

Developing a style that helps others move from a dead stop is an extremely useful skill. Be the one in your group who helps two people entrenched in conflict to see what they have in common, what is needed to move ahead, and how small progress should still be celebrated. This is not done by being a cajoler or a wide-eyed optimist. Rather, it is about someone who has a goal in mind, the dyadic goal of changing a stuck something to a moving something.

Fearless facilitators focus others on what will help them move forward (and they are secretly happy, very happy, that the participants gave them the opportunity to do so publicly).

Like a car in a ditch, it is best to accomplish this by:

- *Assessing the situation:* What happened? Who is hurt? Where is the challenge?

- *Suggesting a plan:* How do we get the wheels to grip? What is at hand that can help us? What dangers might this pose?

- *Enlisting help:* This is not just a case of "who" but also one of "where" to position them, "when" they should engage, making sure they know "why," and—most important—"how."

- *Standing ready to do some heavy lifting yourself:* It is important that they know that you are willing to do some work also. It is not only important that you do the work; you must be seen doing the work.

- *Encouraging the team:* Moving a vehicle or a team from a dead stop is not an easy matter. It requires that they know they can do it. Our colleague Char Wenc from Loyola University teaches that encouragement is what you say to the runners in a marathon as they pass by you; praise is what you reserve for the winner. Encouragement is the nourishment; praise is the celebration. Give more encouragement than you do praise.

- *Celebrating the success:* Never neglect the importance of recognizing the goal achieved, even in small ways (like a handwritten thank you, a sincere voicemail, or even an in-person drop-by).

Keeping Momentum

Helping others keep moving after the initial success and enthusiasm is the real key to successful leadership. Making time to notice the strength in other individuals and the team is a key feature of maintaining momentum. You can render increased progress when you find ways to help people do more.

Two of our friends recently went on a ritzy Mediterranean cruise, with three hundred passengers and a six-hundred-member crew! Within a day of boarding, they noticed that, regardless of the crew member, they were always called by name and their favorite drink was prepared as they entered the bar! Later, they learned that all three hundred passengers' photos were in the crew's quarters. It became a game for the crew to remember everyone's name. The winning crew member won an additional six hours of shore leave! My hunch is that they didn't do it for the win only; they did it because of the light in the passengers' eyes when they were recognized (that is, facilitated).

During his first lecture of the semester to his undergraduate students at Loyola University in Chicago, Kevin gives them a similar assignment to that given to the Mediterranean crew. During the next week, Kevin asks the students to tell three people what they liked, learned, or appreciated about them. This could be the grocery store clerk, a colleague, a parent, or a professor. At the next class, the students tell heart-warming stories about the people whom they otherwise may have only given a smile. We challenge you to try this, too . . . but try it every week! This is a sure-fire way to maintain successful momentum with your team.

When All Else Fails . . . People Who Won't Change, No Matter What

Sometimes, things won't work out. Teams will stay entrenched, individuals will remain intractable, and organizations will lose their zest. When these times come, it may require you to be a bit of a monk. Listen, and stay ready.

Someone has to listen and, in these times, it may only be you. Listening, however, does not mean staying quiet. Say what you notice in a very encouraging way. Here are a few examples:

- "I know we all know this is a tough market and we are at a bit of a standstill. The numbers are not moving as we wish they would. Our meetings, however, are recognizing the factors that will eventually help us. This is an important time for us to stay focused."

- "We have a talented team. We'll figure this out."
- "I love the way we all call it like it is!"

Paraphrasing, empathy, and direct talk are the antidotes of pain between two people. It is very difficult to dialogue with someone and stay in a painful, fearful place. On the other hand, debates can continue for decades! When we respect one another, when we recognize and respect our differences, and when we acknowledge our mutual desire to work out our differences, then we have the basis of "figuring it out."

Mutual respect is key. The famous Chicago psychiatrist Rudolf Dreikurs once commented that the real issue in ongoing conflict is not about what we think it to be. We argue and differ about sex and money, politics, morality, clean apartments, where to go, what you said and what I meant, why I must do this or that, and why you should do this.

The fearless facilitator understands what Dreikurs meant when he said that, in all ongoing conflict, what we are really arguing about is respect. Consider an ongoing significant difference or conflict you have. Regardless of what you were arguing about, how often have you felt:

- My right to decide is being weakened.
- My right to control is being jeopardized by the other person.
- My judgment and my ideas are not being considered.
- My prestige and my status are being questioned.
- My feelings just don't seem to count here.
- I feel unfairly treated by this other person.
- I feel defeated.
- I feel powerless.
- I feel inferior.

When these feelings of disrespect exist, little progress will be made with regard to ending the conflict or bridging the difference. When there is respect, Dreikurs said, any problem can be solved. Without it, we'll simply continue to conflict. Respect levels the playing field.

Know that things will not always go as you wish. Part of the "fearless" part of facilitation is this very point. What does this have to do with facilitation? There will be times in one-to-one or one-to-one-hundred when conflict will occur and you will sense it. Someone may have been offended by something you said (a word, a thought, or a careless gesture). Or you may notice a persistent disagreeableness exists just below the surface. These are times when it may be in your best interest to understand that respect may be the real issue.

Fearless facilitators know that respect may be the only route to resolution, even when nobody else sees it.

Coach's Comments

- How did you learn about the differences in audiences?

The first step is to ask them! Even moments before, preferably days before, ask this question: "If there is one thing that you want to learn/hear/hope for in this presentation/meeting, what would that be?" Don't ask what they want, or what "one thing" they want. This forces deeper learning, you'll receive a more immediate and useful answer, and it actually creates intimacy. In effect, the other thinks, "You really want to know!"

The second step is to watch them. Audiences, when you are aware, are very self-revealing, especially if you train yourself to get off the stage or the riser, move close to them, engage them with your eyes and your liveliness. They will tell you plenty if you will only notice and develop a sixth sense about them.

The third step is to experiment and watch their reactions. Actually, the more you change, move, duck, weave and bob (!), the more they will respond to you. Watch what they respond to, when they nod to you and to their fellow audience members, where they chuckle, when they laugh, when they are moved. We wish there were a magic formula here. We learned it by trusting ourselves with our experiences over time and mostly our awareness.

Fearless facilitators know that awareness is a good thing!

- I work with introverts. How do I encourage them to speak up and enjoy this "group work," work that they say reminds them of middle school?

You may want to spend a good amount of time in pre-work, individually surfacing burning questions and desired solutions. This will help you formulate topics for discussion. You may want to create or articulate an "enemy" . . . "the school board is considering taking a hatchet to our program; we have to have a coordinated strategy." These types of audiences thrive on a task given, not a task discussion. You might also recruit one of them to co-present with you so that one of their own is up in front. Be careful here with your own energy: tone down, don't shout, slow down, and be deliberate and precise.

- I've been asked to present at an academic conference. People don't facilitate there . . . they just read their papers! I don't want to look like a crazy rebel, for I fear losing my reputation. What should I do?

Sometimes you have to understand the culture and abide with it while in a stealthy way facilitating all the way! One thing you might do are some subtle facilitation techniques for academic and scientific conferences:

- Get out from behind the lectern, if only standing next to it.

- Use the stage by moving as you lecture.

- Spice up your PowerPoint by using the "less is more" strategy on your slides.

- Continue to pepper your presentation with words such as:

  "The reason this is important is. . . ."

  "You may want to see what your reaction to this next slide is . . ."

  "I wonder what your university might do with this information."

"Consider for a moment . . . "

"What do you think the person next to you thinks of this?"

"What do you think of this?"

Begin your presentation with the three things you most want them to leave with rather than only the standard "agenda" slide (which no one really pays any attention to anyway).

Throw "meat" out to the audience right away. Don't say who you are (they know that) or where you are from (they know that, too) or how tough it was to get here today (they don't care). Tell them why they should listen, what is in it for them; make it juicy and succinct and powerful.

One researcher began his very scientific lecture simply reciting ten descriptions from his patients of what their disease felt like, one after another. He then said, "What we do today and tomorrow can end that suffering. This is why we are here."

- I only have five minutes with a data-focused director! If I ask what he wants to learn from the meeting, I fear he'll say, "I already told you when we scheduled this meeting! I don't have time for this!" Help!

So did he tell you? It is a good idea to listen to what he said and what he didn't say. Give him what he wants early and often. If you truly don't know, then don't ask a vague question like "What do you want?" or "Please don't hurt me!" Try this one instead, "What are three things you most need from my data?" or "You're going upstairs with this data. What do you think they want?" Mostly don't be afraid. Data-minded directors hate that! Be confident, even when they yell. Remember, don't fight, don't give in; but stand up for yourself at least visually.

No fear!

Eleven

Conclusion: Now Is the Beginning of Your New Skill

"It's all about engagement! At the beginning, I try to get a sense of who they are and what's important to them. Judicious use of relevant videos or humor helps draw participants in as well."

—*Walter Eppich, MD, M.Ed., Northwestern University Feinberg School of Medicine*

AND SO WE HAVE COME to the end of our journey of fearlessness. This is the real key to facilitating, presenting, working with colleagues, customers, perhaps even at home. Adler once remarked that, if he were to give a child any personality characteristic, he would give the characteristic of courage. For with courage one can combat life's greatest problem, which is fear.

Fearless facilitators know they can do this! And we think you can also!

Appendix A:
Sure Things: Eight Discussion
Topics That Never Fail

TO BE TRULY FEARLESS, YOU'LL need some tools on your belt that work every time with every audience . . . guaranteed!

The following topics can be used as icebreakers or can tie into other topics and ideas throughout the presentation. These are guaranteed in that we have *never seen them fail*—with any and all audiences.

1. What was a favorite childhood pastime, and how does it still represent you and your style today? We have used this in executive retreats as the icebreaker. It equalizes everyone beautifully. Modifications include asking them to tie the childhood pastime into their leadership styles today or their presentation styles today, etc.

2. Describe your most memorable "first day on the job." This is often either hilarious or sadly pathetic. People have said they sat in an empty office all day and nobody acknowledged them.

3. Describe your best or worst boss and tell what you learned from him or her. While a commonly used topic, the key here is to probe for detail and to persuade the rest of the group to comment on what others say.

4. What do you learn most from your pet? How many pets do you own? Who has the most unusual pet? What do you wish you could do that your pet does? Most audience members today are pet owners. Those who are not can often comment on a childhood pet or a significant other's pet. It's easy to tie pet characteristics to themes of people skills, team building, stress, time, work balance, and communication.

5. What makes you angry? or What's your pet peeve? Don't use this one as an icebreaker, but later in the program when you can tie it into a difficult issue you may be discussing. Dale Carnegie began his speaking career with this question back in the 1930s; he found it was the one question *everyone* could talk about without hesitation.

6. What is your birth order in the family? What has that taught you? We find this discovery helpful when discussing just about any communication, influence, or conflict issues. It's fun to break the group into small groups based on birth order, but this can also be processed in partner discussions.

7. What are your biggest time-wasters? This is a good question for time and life management presentations, but it also works very well to discuss almost anything: project management, customer service excellence, employee productivity, management, leadership, sales, etc.

8. What would you tell a new hire about how to succeed in your field? Anyone and everyone who has worked in a job role even a few months figures out how to succeed. This question is good for retreats, team building, sales meetings, service training, and many other situations.

Appendix B:
Four Keys to Making It Easier

HERE IS SOME MORE ON the mindset, the approach, the skill, and the follow-up that make skilled facilitators impactful and more memorable
than slide-deck-only presenters.

The Mindset

The fearless facilitator's job is not about the PowerPoint slide deck or about
himself or herself as the content expert. It is rather about a mindset that is
completely audience-experience focused.

This is no easy task in a corporate culture that stresses perfection, com-
pletion, and robust slide decks to be read rather than presented.

Your mindset will make the difference—the critical difference. Consider
when you are speaking with someone who is distracted or feels he or she is

right or who wants to dominate you or one who is even somewhat disengaged. Are you aware immediately that something is "off"? On the other hand, think about those times of complete engagement when you are speaking to someone. He or she is on heightened alert, paying attention, listening, with a complete focus.

Fearless facilitators are akin to this listener. They sharpen their mindsets in at least three ways:

1. They prepare with a laser-like singular purpose directed toward the audience experience, not just the presenter content for the audience.

2. They proceed confidently and literally wade into the audience, both physically and psychologically. They take control of the meeting in order to provide the experience that is the ultimate goal.

3. They reflect the views of the "other" so as to combine those views with the community before them. They are not unlike a chef with ingredients needing to be combined, seasoned, mixed again, tasted, and presented.

The Approach

Like the mindset, the approach of the fearless facilitator is one without ego, of service, and one-to-one in terms of presence, eye contact, consultation, and conversation. Like a new couple making the rounds of the tables at a wedding reception, so too the fearless facilitator is the ultimate busy bee, knowing that to do the work well means to be present and have presence, to understand and be understood, and to engage others with hospitality, warmth, and curiosity.

In effect, the fearless facilitator is everywhere at once and nowhere in particular. We have equated fearless facilitators with Montessori teachers, not at the forefront, but leading; not the focus, but in charge of the experience; not the boss, but the leader.

If you were to watch the ultimate fearless facilitator, you would see him or her presenting briefly, giving simple and clear directions for interaction, moving smoothly around the room as the groups talk. You'd even see him or her picking up old coffee cups, moving chairs, posting flip-chart paper, and having quick, focused private conversations both verbally and non-verbally . . . all the while knowing that each intentional move, even with coffee cups, moves the group toward the experience.

When attendees walk into our room we want them to be a bit of disoriented. "No tables?" When we begin, and within minutes, they are working in small groups, for we want them to have a bit of "We don't usually do this!" on their minds. When we move them from group to group, we do want them to have the experience of "I just met someone interesting!" As they leave we want them to think, feel, and say, "That was different . . . better . . . really good!"

The Skill

You will need three critical skills that are ever-evolving, never complete, and will serve you very well in every situation:

1. Listen like never before with total focus and a relentless spirit of inquiry. Refuse to be distracted by thinking when the other is talking. Listen instead.

2. Pause and think before you respond. Even better, ask a question, especially when you think you are right. Being pretty sure you are right is a distinct warning sign that you are about to veer off course.

3. Be willing to take a risk, not a wild chance, but a calculated risk based on conviction and courage devoted solely for the benefit of the audience experience. They've never done small groups before? Put them in small groups. Never had a venue with chairs only? Insist on it. Never had a one-on-one interview? Do it. If anyone should take a risk, it should be you. Your audience needs you to be the one.

The Follow-Up

This is where the wheels can come off the train! Many presenters take a bow and leave. Fearless facilitators see the ending of their time with the group as a commencement, a beginning, not an end.

Make sure that you are allowing them room to grow beyond your time with them. Send them articles, write some yourself, keep in touch with education, not promotion. Continue to monitor them and their leadership.

Because of the group's experience with you, you will be seen as someone special to them and, in a sense, you will become a kind of brand or trademark for that day you had with them.

We often have attendees coming up to us literally years later saying "Remember that time in Puerto Rico? What a meeting that was!" This is not a testament to us personally as much as it is to what we allowed to happen because of our mindset, the approach, the skills we use, and the follow-up we provide. This is the mission, the work, even the leadership that fearless facilitators provide.

Appendix C:
Momentum Magic

THIS IS ABOUT HOW TO keep things going, especially when they are going very well, and knowing when to stop just in the nick of time before too much is too much!

Twenty keys to momentum magic:

1. They want the *experience* of you and the content.

2. *Simple* is better than contrived.

3. *Listen* to what they give you and comment, compliment.

4. Give directions in steps, with a light tone, *very clear, nonthreatening,* and *quick.*

5. Be among them when you have interaction.

6. Find *volunteers* as you're among them; *prepare* them for sharing with the group.

7. Think *dialogue* when you're out among them; keep the *conversation* going; tie in points.

8. Use one *partner* activity, one group of *three*, and one *in-the-front* interview or demo.

9. *Stop* when they're not quite done; they'll still be thinking as you move on.

10. *Trust* the organic feel.

11. Use a sports or household *analogy* to explain a concept; get the audience involved.

12. *Interview* an audience member in front of the group for at least one minute.

13. Ask the group to *recall* an experience as a leader or volunteer when they were in high school.

14. Incorporate a short dance step or *movement* routine into your program. Involve the audience. Make sure it emphasizes a concept.

15. Form into *partners* and do something quickly.

16. Ask a *question* that makes someone feel proud of what he or she does.

17. Open the presentation *from the back* of the room.

18. Ask someone to *come up front* and do something with you.

19. Show pictures or a *prop*.

20. Have the *least- and most*-experienced persons in the room stand up and answer a question.

You will note that none of these ideas is laden with technique or intense instructions. The key in maintaining momentum is to remember you're on a long-distance run . . . not a sprint! You have to keep the energy sustained and the spirit lively.

Appendix D:
Oops! When Meetings Don't Go So Well

MANY FACILITATORS TELL US they would like to be better "thinking on their feet"—especially with unanticipated difficult people and questions. What can they do to help their brains to "kick in" when under stress? How can they quickly select the right answers? How can they persuade others to agree with their responses?

This true story shared by a neighbor inspired our own thinking around quick thinking—where it starts and how it is played out: The neighbor's son and his young teen friends were having fun on Chicago's Navy Pier one cold winter night. They had walked to the edge of the pier and were watching the waves, having left their backpacks in a pile nearby. But the fun was short-lived. One of them was too close and an unanticipated wind gust knocked him into the freezing cold Lake Michigan water. The other friends, shocked and frightened, began screaming for help—frantically trying to pull him back on the pier, but the sides were slippery and high and he was unable to get a grip.

And that's when, out of courage and uncanny quick thinking, our neighbor's fourteen-year-old son ran to the pile of backpacks, grabbed one, and tied his sweatshirt to it; then, holding the pack and extending the tied-on arm of the shirt, he was able to help the friend in the water take hold. After some struggle, all the boys finally pulled him up and out, using the backpack as the needed leverage.

This story was shared with great modesty, but we know that his son, the youngest of five children raised in urban Chicago, was taught the values of self-reliance and discipline that life in the big city dictates. Quick thinking doesn't just come from nowhere. Quick thinking comes from years of listening and learning and self-reliance. Most likely the boy's actions were in some way a result of those years and values.

Now, facilitating rarely requires life saving, but it may require us to think fast in a tense, stressful, or awkward atmosphere. So the best way to prepare is to listen, learn, practice, and accept that we have an appropriate response within us . . . in our own "backpacks"! If we master audience focus and forget our egos, it's easier to have that "backpack" ready when the wave hits.

So what should be in your "backpack"?

- *Ego-less attitude*. Let go of your ego and work to maintain your professionalism. You will be much more respected if you present yourself as an equal who is simply ready to steer the ship.

- *Courageous questions*. Be honest and ask the group what they sense is happening and what they would like to do about it.

- *Quick-moving decision*. Whatever you do, do something! Make a statement, stretch, write on the whiteboard, take a break, ask for a show of hands—anything that moves the awkwardness forward.

- *Kind control.* Don't allow the angry, hurt, or evil person to take over your meeting. Honestly tell the truth: "This is a heated point; let's rest it for now and talk on the side" might be an example of a phrase you would use.

- *Relish the moment.* You can enjoy the unexpected if you combine a sense of wonder, a sense of humor, a sense of ordinary curiosity, and a keen eye toward the audience, not an eye trained inward!

Kevin was in the midst of teaching his graduate students on the first day with his co-teacher. As the students went around the room, one from India introduced himself with his first name only. Kevin had seen the roster and knew his last name had eighteen letters to it! Kevin said, "How do you pronounce your last name?" The student smiled and spoke a bit about his region of India and then said something that the other students laughed at. Kevin wears hearing aids and every once in a while he misses a comment or two. As he did this time! When the laughter died down, Kevin said, "So how do you pronounce it?" His co-teacher said, "He just told us!" More laughter! Kevin said later that, at that moment, he had a flash of embarrassment that he tempered knowing that the moment was good for the group.

Know, too, when part of the learning is the pain that the meeting might bring. This pain is not about you, but about them. Allow them to experience it so you can help guide them through it. Your job is not to make it easy for them; your job is to make the meeting easy in order to discover.

Appendix E:
Techniques for Teleconference and Virtual Meeting Facilitation

HERE'S THE GOOD NEWS: nearly everything you have read in this book applies to virtual meetings. Some techniques you facilitate exactly the same—others slightly differently. But you are aiming for the same result—audience involvement! Here are some guidelines:

1. Get to know your virtual audience just as you would your live audience. E-mail, call, text, or survey them prior to the meeting. Encourage them to respond with brief but pointed answers, and ask them what their goals are. In addition to providing valuable information, this will give you a sense of who is most committed to the outcome. It will also give you material to refer to during your call or virtual meeting.

2. You also can "break the fourth wall" as the "live" facilitator does by encouraging comments right away. After you deliver the opening purpose and objectives, involve everyone!

3. Use pre- and post-work to your advantage. While you can't have partner and small group discussions in quite the same way, you can suggest pre-work and post-work to be completed with partners or small groups, who can then report their findings during the meeting. For virtual meetings, it is possible to ask groups of people to "chat" online.

4. Use a headset so that your voice is clear and strong.

5. Stand up when you speak! Yes, even if you are all alone! Again, your voice will be heard differently.

6. Have a mirror on your desk and "consult your smile" frequently. It will be "heard" with your voice. Otherwise something else will be heard!

7. Use your hands when you speak. Your headset will help here. You will sound more animated.

8. Use notes . . . but don't read them word for word.

9. Tell your audience that anytime anyone has a question to simply press any phone key and you will stop and request the input. When you do, find out their names and locations. Don't be afraid to ask a quick question about the weather, best restaurant in their town, and so forth, as a way to loosen up the group. It will pay off big time in terms of interest and rapport.

10. As Dr. Walter Eppich recommends, be explicit when you ask a question. "I need you to; I want you to; Please join in now with your comment. . . ." Remember that they only have your voice and perhaps a PowerPoint slide to keep them focused. And they have plenty to keep them unfocused (e-mails, babies, dogs, and eating, to name only a few!).

Index

the conversation in new direction, 31–32; single-focused, 139–140; trusting your, 74, 75, 133; understanding mindset of, 36; unexpectedly small audience, 56–57; very large, 54–56; when you are the wrong presenter for the, 140–142; when your expertise doesn't match needs of the, 139–140

Avoiding death by committee, 126–127

B

Bellman, Geoff, 73

Bentley University (Massachusetts), 88

Berra, Yogi, 111

Bias, 110–111

Bierce, Dianna, 93

"Bingo time" metaphor, 117–119

Bon Jovi, Jon, 58

Boosler, Elayne, 124

Breaks, 65–66

"Burning questions," 22, 23, 30

C

Cain, Susan, 62

Campbell, Susan, 79

"Career day talk" experience, 120

Carlin, George, 123

Carnegie, Dale, 62

Carson, Johnny, 123

Chapman, Gary, 25

Chicago magazine, 119

"Chunking" content: Kevin's "lecturettes" for, 59; mini-lectures for, 7, 23

City University (Hong Kong), 102

Clooney, George, 140

Closed-ended questions, 94

Coach's Comments: avoid using "planted questions," 29–30; on breaking down the "fourth wall," 42–43; on difficult questions and situations, 105–106; on facilitation role in every speaking engagement, 16–17; on facilitator role as educator, 29; on "gently" setting-up fearless facilitation, 80–83; on handling differences in audiences, 150–152; on having fun, 57–60; on how to go with it!, 113–114; on how to prepare to facilitate, 32; on knowing when to present and when to facilitate, 30–31; on process of organic facilitation, 29–32; on strategies for having fun regarding of audience size, 57–60; on successful conversations with dominators, 67–70

Columbia College Chicago, 114, 127, 140

"Columbo moments," 100–101

Comedians: five things to learn from, 124; what they know about engaging an audience, 123–124

Comedy Store (Los Angeles), 124

Commencement speech, 76

Communication: and facilitating through any circumstances, 75–77; "the five love languages" of marital, 25–26; horizontal, 12–13; vertical, 12; what the best do not do, 88–89. *See also* Listening; Nonverbal communication

Complication questions, 97

Conflict: anger leading to, 144–145; maintaining mutual respect during, 149–150; understanding that there may be, 148–150. *See also* Fight-or-flight reactions

Connecting: content trumped by, 2–3, 6; the difference between seeking perfection and,